The Gentleman's Guide to Cooking

RANDY MOTILALL

To order additional copies of this book, contact:
Xlibris
844-714-8691
www.Xlibris.com
Orders@Xlibris.com

In Partnership with HOD Productions, LLC
Photography: Randy Motilall
Cover Photography: L.R. Westeen Photography
Photography Editing & Enhancements by: L. R. Westeen
Photography

ISBN: Softcover   978-1-6641-5904-4
       Hardcover   978-1-6641-5905-1
       EBook   978-1-6641-5903-7

Library of Congress Control Number: 2021903564

Print information available on the last page

Rev. date: 02/19/2021

Dedication

I would like to dedicate this book to my parents. My parents came to the United States in 1981 from Guyana, South America, with nothing but seventy-five dollars in their pockets and four suitcases. My parents have worked every day of their lives for the past forty-one years of being in the states. They have worked so hard to give my brothers, sister, and I every opportunity we could ever dream of in life. They taught us a lot of valuable life lessons that I have used in everyday life and been able to develop into gentlemanly qualities.

From a young age, my parents always encouraged me to cook at home and never deterred me from making anything. If it were not for my parents, I would not be where I am today and would not have accomplished what I have in my life to this day. The opportunities my parents have provided me with have allowed me to travel the world, pursue an education that has led to a successful career in the medical industry, and fuel my passion to cook to my heart's desire. Therefore, this book is for you, Mom and Dad.

Foreword

Living between Minneapolis and Los Angeles during my late twenties and early thirties had always made it challenging to keep up with friends from college, especially at an age when significant changes in one's life could happen in a very short time. The common denominator that brought us men and fraternity brothers together had always been food. We had all excelled in our prospective fields and naturally graduated from breaking bread from your typical college chains to indulging in the finest meals money could buy, ranging from the finest cuts of meat to freshly imported seafood.

I began to feel a subtle shift in our behavior. The frequency of restaurant visits gradually began to lessen and was substituted with home-cooked meals at Randy's. It became a habit to land in Minneapolis on Thursday evenings and get dropped off at Randy's home for dinner. Our cravings for fine foods and triggering flavors were consistently met, along with the indulgence of a classy ambience. Randy's altruistic nature and sharp attention to detail had allowed him to create detailed recipes for high-end meals that could be achieved at the price of affordable ingredients. Prior to knowing a book was in the process of being developed, Randy would be asking for genuine feedback after meals were consumed; and most of the time, I'd look back with a wink and gesture the perfect symbol. It wasn't until recently that I asked for his recipe to the braised beef short rib, a meal that he prepared with extreme perfection causing for the short rib to dissolve in your mouth within seconds of a bite. To my surprise, his response was "You'll have to wait for the book."

I am beyond proud and excited for Randy to have his book of recipes accessible to the world. Who knows, maybe one day we can all dine at an establishment called Randy's.

Ahmed Mawas
Actor, producer, cybersecurity expert

Preface

Welcome to *The Gentleman's Guide to Cooking*, an accessible yet elevated introduction to making impressive creations in your own home. Let me start by saying that the word "gentleman" does not mean what you think it means. While I have been known to don a suit and sip classic cocktails, being a gentleman is so much more than that. It is about how you carry yourself. Regardless of gender, job, or location, we can all tap our inner gentleman to enjoy life a little bit more.

My cooking adventure began where many do: as a kid in my parents' kitchen. Growing up in a Caribbean household in the United States, I worked with a variety of spices and ingredients to invent my own recipes. I especially enjoyed watching my parents cook outdoors for large family gatherings, realizing that amazing food could be created anytime, anywhere. I learned the valuable lesson of using my own hands to deliver mouthwatering creations. I remember going to restaurants and, after one bite, hearing my mom say, "I can make that." And you know what, she almost always could. Watching my parents recreate meals motivated me to also experiment and tackle different dishes when I stepped into my very own kitchen.

My inspiration for this cookbook came during the 2020 global pandemic; for almost a decade, my work travel as a medical consultant allowed me to indulge in different dining experiences before I was, quite literally, grounded. I found myself reflecting on opportunities lost and cuisine unconsumed while traveling and dining out, as did others in my life. I began remaking some of my favorite classics and adding some twists to mix it up. As I posted images of my reimagined meals on social media, I received an unexpected wave of likes, shares, and glowing comments. I also had many requests for recipes from family, friends, and even friends of friends. As I began sharing my creations, I also added in tips and tricks for emulating an upscale experience. I wanted to make sure that what they saw would be what they got. I walked them through everything from pan heat to plating, helping loved ones to love the meals they serve.

The Gentleman's Guide to Cooking is for anyone who wants to be impressive but not pretentious while serving jaw-dropping food without dropping big bucks in the process. From handcrafted cocktails to sesame-ginger tuna tartare, to seared spiced lamb chops, to glazed donut bread pudding, my step-by-step instructions will get you cooking and plating in a way to be proud of. The dishes I have created may not be quick, instant meals. Rather they are well-crafted dishes from around the world. Although a recipe list may seem intimidating, don't be discouraged. I have always said that surrounding yourself with the right ingredients is like surrounding yourself with the right people; a gentleman always makes the right choice.

No matter your skill level in the kitchen, anyone can create these dishes with a little patience and willingness to take a chance on something new to impress their guest or date. So let's make plans for dinner, and let me walk you through creating an elegant dining experience.

Table Setting

An integral part to any dining experience is sitting down to a properly laid out table setting. Think about when you go to a nice restaurant: while you have certainly come for the food and company, the table setting itself is the first thing you see when you approach your seats. To create the desired welcoming environment, everything is in pristine condition, hopefully encouraging the diners to feel comfortable for the evening ahead.

Knowing how to set a formal table setting is a skill all gentlemen and hosts should understand and embrace. This shows you are willing to go the extra mile for your guests and ensures they will have an enjoyable meal to remember. A formal table setting includes many pieces: dinner plate; soup/salad bowl; bread plate; different types of knives, forks, spoons; and an arrangement of drinking glasses for the occasion.

With so many pieces, it can be daunting, but here is a basic layout for a formal table setting. Each course of your meal will require a different plate and utensil, so set your table based on what you will be serving for the evening. The idea is to arrange your table setting utensils in the order in which they will be used for the dining experience.

1- Dinner plate
2- Soup or salad bowl
3- Bread plate
4- Water glass
5- Red wine glass
6- White wine glass
7- Dinner fork
8- Salad fork
9- Dinner knife
10- Dessert spoon
11- Soup spoon
12- Butter knife
13- Table napkin
14- Salt and pepper shakers

Contents

APPETIZERS

Beef and Lamb Kabobs

Beef and Lamb Kabobs
(yields 10–12 kabobs)
1 LB ground beef
1 LB ground lamb
4–5 cloves garlic (minced)
1 TBS chives (minced)
1 medium jalapeño (seeded and minced)
1 large egg
½ tsp garlic powder
½ tsp onion powder
¼ tsp cumin
¼ tsp paprika
¼ tsp white pepper
¼ tsp cayenne pepper
¼ tsp dill
½ tsp salt
¼ tsp black pepper
¼ tsp sumac

⅛ tsp ground nutmeg
¼ tsp ground allspice

Tzatziki Sauce
1½ C plain Greek yogurt
½ English cucumber (peeled and grated)
1 tsp minced garlic
1 TBS fresh lemon juice
1 TBS olive oil
2 TBS fresh dill (chopped)
½ tsp salt

Toum (Garlic Sauce)
½ C fresh peeled garlic
2 C canola oil
¼ C fresh lemon juice
salt

Kabobs
1) In a large bowl, combine ground beef, ground lamb, garlic, chives, jalapeño, and egg. Mix together until uniform.
2) Next, add garlic powder, onion powder, cumin, paprika, white pepper, cayenne pepper, dill, salt, black pepper, sumac, nutmeg, and allspice to bowl. Mix all together until seasonings are incorporated into meat mixture.
3) Cover and refrigerate for 1 hour.
4) To prepare kabobs, split mixture into 10–12 equal portions (roughly 1.5 oz each). Using hands, form a cylinder shape with meat that is about 4 inches long. Insert skewer into cylinder and set aside. Repeat until all kabobs are formed.
5) Place a large skillet over medium heat. Place 3–4 kabobs into skillet and cook for 2–3 minutes. Turn kabobs over and cook other side for 2–3 minutes. Remove from heat and set aside. Repeat until all kabobs are cooked.

Tzatiki Sauce
1) Grate peeled English cucumber and place in a towel or cheesecloth and ring out excess water.
2) In a medium-sized bowl, add yogurt, cucumber, garlic, lemon juice, olive oil, dill, and salt. Mix together until uniform. If desired, add more salt to taste.
   (Sauce can be refrigerated for about 2 weeks.)

Toum
1) Add peeled garlic and salt to food processor. Process the garlic and salt until a smooth consistency is formed. You may need to stop and scrape sides of food processor a couple of times.
2) Next, while food processor is running, slowly add 1 cup of canola oil.
3) Once canola oil is incorporated, slowly add lemon juice to food processor. Then add remaining 1 cup of canola oil.
4) You should have a smooth, fluffy white mixture. Adjust salt level to taste.
5) Place sauce in a bowl and cover with a damp paper towel and place in the refrigerator for a minimum of 6 hours before serving.

Bacon-Wrapped Shrimp

8 large shrimp (peeled and deveined)
3 strips of bacon
2 TBS honey

2 TBS maple syrup
1 TBS garlic chili paste
pinch of black pepper

1) Preheat oven to 400°F.
2) Cut bacon strips into ⅓s. Wrap each shrimp with a ⅓ of bacon. Secure bacon with a toothpick.
3) In a small bowl, combine honey, maple syrup, garlic chili paste, and black pepper. Mix together.
4) Line a baking sheet with aluminum foil. Place shrimp on baking sheet. Using a brush, coat each shrimp with a few strokes of glaze on both sides. Reserve excess glaze.
5) Place glaze coated shrimp into oven and bake for 20 minutes.
6) Remove shrimp from oven. Turn broiler on in oven to high.
7) Using remaining glaze, coat each shrimp again. Place back in oven and broil for 2 minutes.
8) Remove from oven and serve.

Bruschetta and Mushroom Crostini

Mushroom Crostini
(yields 6 pieces)

4 oz small white mushroom (sliced)
4 oz small baby bella mushroom (sliced)
½ tsp minced garlic
2 tsp fresh oregano (finely chopped)
1 tsp fresh thyme (finely chopped)
2 TBS butter
¼ tsp salt
¼ tsp black pepper
1 TBS fresh chives (chopped)
4 oz crème fraîche

Bruschetta
(yields 6 pieces)

1½ C Roma tomato (diced)

1 tsp minced garlic
8 large fresh basil leaves
⅛ tsp salt
⅛ tsp black pepper
1½ tsp olive oil
2 tsp balsamic glaze
2 TBS shredded Parmesan cheese

Additional Items
1 large loaf of French bread
1 large garlic clove
olive oil

Bruschetta
1) Layer basil leaves on top of one another and roll together vertically and tightly. Slice basil into thin strips.
2) In a large bowl, combine tomato, garlic, basil, and Parmesan cheese. Mix together. Next, add olive oil and balsamic glaze to bowl and mix together with other ingredients.
3) Lastly, add salt and pepper. Mix together. If desired, add more salt and pepper to taste.

Mushroom Crostini
1) Place a pan on stove over medium heat. Add cleaned white baby bella mushrooms to pan. Cook for 6–7 minutes, stirring occasionally.
2) Once water has cooked down in mushrooms, lower heat to medium-low. Add thyme, oregano, garlic, and butter and stir together until butter is melted and has coated mushrooms (for about 5 minutes).
3) Add salt and pepper. Mix together. If desired, add additional salt and pepper to taste.

Preparing Toast
1) Place a skillet on stove over medium-high.
2) Cut French bread into ½ inch slices. Brush on side of bread with olive oil.
3) Place oiled side of bread down on skillet and toast bread until golden brown (about 1–1½ minutes).
4) Peel large garlic clove and cut in half.
5) Once bread is toasted, remove from skillet; and while toast is warm, rub onto toast the cut side of garlic clove to infuse garlic.

Serving

Bruschetta: Using a large tablespoon, add about 1–1½ TBS of bruschetta mixture to each piece of toast. Finish with a drizzle of olive oil.

Mushroom crostini: Using a spoon, spread ½ TBS of crème fraîche to each piece of toast. Add 1–1½ TBS of mushroom mixture to each piece of toast. Finish with sprinkle of fresh chives.

Chicken Taco-Wonton Cups

Chicken Tacos
1 LB skinless-boneless chicken
  breast (cut into ¼ inch cubes)
1 TBS chili powder
½ tsp garlic powder
½ tsp onion powder
¼ tsp crushed red pepper flake
¼ tsp dried oregano
½ tsp paprika
1 tsp ground cumin
1 tsp salt
½ tsp white pepper
½ tsp black pepper
1 TBS canola oil
½ TBS water
16 square wonton wrappers
cooking spray

Salsa Taquera
2 large Roma tomatoes

1 medium white onion (roughly chopped)
4–6 dried chile de arbol
3 large cloves garlic
6 TBS canola oil
½ tsp salt

Aji Verde
¾ C Mexican crema
2 C lightly packed cilantro
3 medium jalapeños (seeds and
  membranes removed; chopped)
3 cloves garlic (chopped)
⅓ C cotija
1 TBS lime juice
¼ tsp salt

Additional Toppings
fresh pico de gallo
extra cotija

Chicken Taco
1) Preheat oven to 375°F.
2) In a large bowl, add chicken, water, chili powder, garlic powder, onion powder, crushed red pepper, oregano, paprika, cumin, salt, white pepper, and black pepper. Mix together until chicken is coated.
3) Place a large pan on stove over medium heat. Add canola oil to pan. Add seasoned chicken to the pan and cook for 5 minutes or until chicken begins to brown. Remove from heat.
4) Use a mini muffin tin; using cooking spray, grease each well of muffin tin. Next, gently press wonton wrappers into muffin tins. Once cups are formed, lightly spray each wonton wrapper with cooking spray (this will help the wonton wrappers to crisp).
5) Spoon in about 1 TBS of cooked chicken into each wonton cup.
6) Place in the oven and bake for 15–20 minutes. Remove from oven when edges of wonton wrapper begin to brown. Allow to cool for 5 minutes.
7) Remove cups from muffin tin and place on platter. Garnish each cup with fresh pico de gallo and cotija.

Salsa Taquera
1) Slice each tomato into 4 halves.
2) Place a medium-sized pan on stove over medium-high heat. Add 2 TBS canola oil to pan. Add tomatoes and onions to pan and cook for 5 minutes, stirring occasionally.
3) Add garlic to pan and cook for 2 minutes with tomatoes and onions.
4) Remove stems from chile de arbol and add to pan and cook for 1 minute. *Do not cook chiles longer*; they could burn.
5) Transfer all ingredients to blender and blend together for 30.
6) While still blending, add remaining canola oil to blender. Blend for an additional minute or until salsa has smooth, thick consistency.
7) Adjust with salt if needed.

Aji Verde
1) Add crema, cilantro, jalapeños, garlic, cotija, lime juice, and salt to blender.
2) Blend together until a smooth consistency is formed. Stop and scrape down sides of blender to ensure all ingredients have been incorporated.
3) Adjust with salt if needed.

Vegetarian Alternative
If you wish to make this a vegetarian appetizer, substitute 1 LB of portobello mushrooms in place of chicken. Cook mushrooms until softened.

Sesame-Ginger Tuna Tartare

Guacamole
1 TBS jalapeño (seeded and diced)
1 C English cucumber (peeled
   and cut into small cubes)
½ C cilantro (finely chopped)
1 large avocado (cut into small cubes)
1½ TBS pomegranate seeds
1 TBS lime juice
salt and pepper

Tuna Tartare
8 oz tuna (cut into small ¼"–½" cubes)
3 scallions (thinly sliced)

1 TBS toasted white sesame seeds
1 TBS toasted black sesame seeds

Sauce
2 cloves garlic (minced)
1 TBS grated ginger
1 TBS soy sauce
1 TBS sesame oil
1 TBS honey
1 TBS rice wine vinegar
1 tsp red pepper flake (optional)

1) In a large bowl, combine jalapeño, cucumber, cilantro, avocado, and lime juice and toss together. Add salt and pepper to taste. Be sure not to mash avocados.
2) In a separate bowl, combine tuna, scallions, and sesame seeds.
3) In a third bowl, combine garlic, ginger, soy sauce, sesame oil, honey, rice wine vinegar, and red pepper flake (optional). Stir together until all ingredients are combined.
4) Add sauce mixture to tuna mixture. Toss together and allow to marinade for 20–30 minutes.
5) Place ring mold in center of serving plate.
6) Fill half of the ring mold with guacamole mixture and lightly press mixture into mold, ensuring not to mash avocado-cucumber mixture.
7) Next, add tuna tartare mixture to ring mold and layer on top of guacamole layer. Lightly press tartare into ring mold.
8) Allow layers to settle in ring mold for 3–4 minutes.
9) Gently and slowly lift the ring mold from the plate in an upward motion until ring mold is free of tartare.
10) Serve with corn tortilla chips.

DRINKS

The Lady Slipper

1¾ oz citrus vodka
3 oz pink lemonade
½ tsp lime juice
1 dash half-and-half milk

¼ C ice
½ C white granulated sugar

- Add ice, vodka, lemonade, lime juice, and half-and-half to cocktail shaker. Place lid on shaker and shake for 10 seconds.
- Pour sugar into a small sauce plate. Using a lime wedge, rub the rim of glass all the way around. Dip rim of glass into sugar to coat.
- Pour from top of cocktail shaker and strain drink into glass.

La Señorita

¾ oz silver tequila
½ lemon juice
chilled sparkling wine

¼ C ice
½ C white granulated sugar

- Add ice, tequila, and lemon juice to cocktail shaker. Using a spoon, mix ingredients together to combine.
- Pour sugar into a small sauce plate. Using a lemon wedge, rub the rim of glass all the way around. Dip rim of glass into sugar to coat.
- Place strainer top onto cocktail shaker. Pour contents into glass. Top off glass with sparkling wine. Use spoon to gently mix drink together.

The Bittersweet

1¾ oz gin
¾ oz triple sec
1¾ oz orange juice
¾ oz pineapple juice

¼ C ice
orange peel garnish

- Add ice, gin, triple sec, orange juice, and pineapple juice to cocktail shaker. Place lid on shaker and shake for 10 seconds.
- Pour from top of cocktail shaker and strain drink into glass. Add orange peel twist for garnish.

The Berbice Breeze

1¾ oz El Dorado 15 Year Old Rum
3 oz pineapple-ginger beer
½ tsp lime juice

¼ C ice
lime slice

- Add ice, rum, pineapple-ginger beer, and lime juice to cocktail shaker. Using a spoon, stir to combine ingredients.
- Add large ice cubes to glass.
- Place strainer top onto cocktail shaker. Pour contents into glass. Garnish with lime slice.

Smoked Old-Fashioned

½ tsp white granulated sugar
3 dashes Angostura bitters
1 tsp water
2 oz bourbon

¼ C ice
lemon peel garnish
2–3 Luxardo cherries

- Add ice, sugar, water, bourbon, and Angostura bitters to cocktail shaker. Using a spoon, stir ingredients together.
- Add large ice cube(s) to glass.
- Pour from top of cocktail shaker and strain drink into glass.
- Place Luxardo cherries on cocktail pick and place in glass and add lemon peel for garnish.

For smoked old-fashioned, place prepared drink inside smokebox. Add cherrywood chips to smoking gun and light. Allow smoke to fill chamber until you can no longer see cocktail glass. Allow smoke to sit for 45 seconds–1 minute. Remove cover from smokebox and serve. If you do not have a smokebox, place hose of smoking gun over glass and cover glass with plastic wrap to seal in smoke. Smoke for 30 seconds and remove place wrap.

BREAD

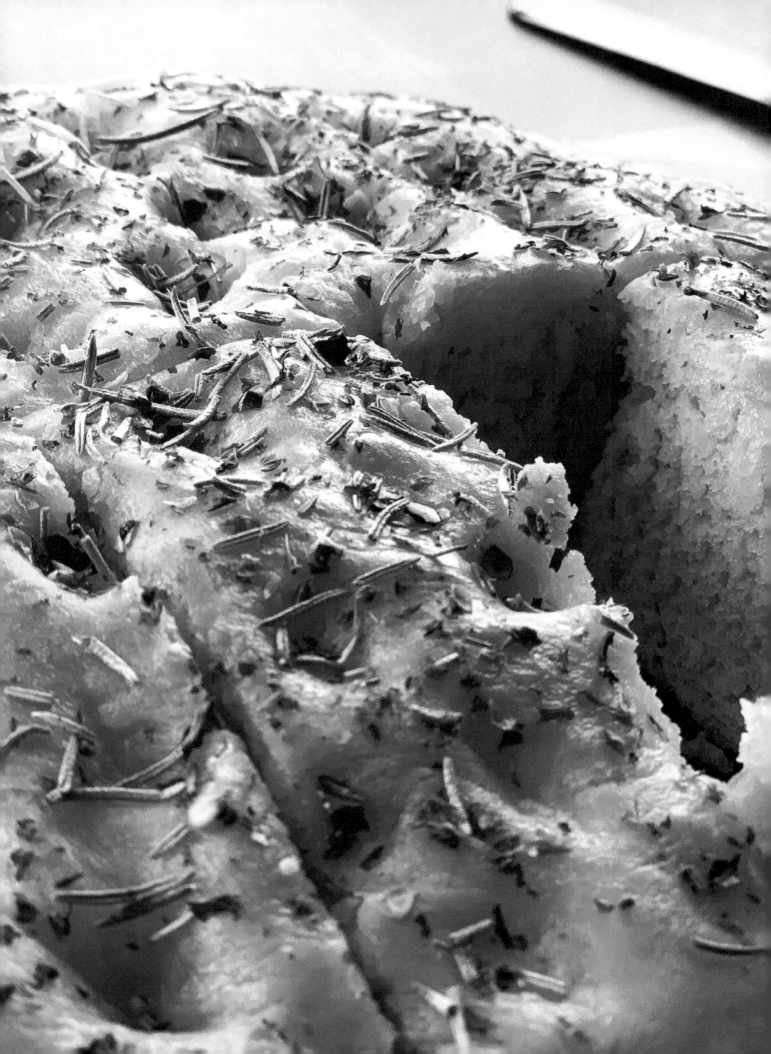

Focaccia Bread

¾ C warm water (90°F)
1 packet active dry yeast
1¾ C all-purpose flour
1 tsp kosher salt
5 TBS olive oil

1 tsp dried rosemary
½ tsp dried oregano
⅛ tsp dried red pepper flake
½ tsp dried parsley

1) Bloom yeast in ¾ C warm water for 5 minutes (let bubbles form). (If water is too hot, it will kill yeast.)
2) Add salt, 1 TBS olive oil, and 1½ C flour to yeast mixture and mix with spatula until fully incorporated.
3) Once mixed together, turn over onto floured surface and knead for 10 minutes or until smooth ball is formed. Add remaining ¼ C of flour to dough 1 TBS at a time or until dough is no longer sticky in texture. (Don't use mixer.)
4) Add 1 TBS olive oil to 10-inch cast-iron skillet and coat bottom of skillet.
5) Add kneaded dough to skillet and stretch out dough to sides of skillet.
6) Cover with towel and let rest at room temperature in skillet for 1–1½ hours or until it doubles in size.
7) Once rested, use fingertips to make light divots in top of dough; *do not press hard into dough.*
8) Add 2 TBS olive oil to top of dough.
9) Sprinkle rosemary, oregano, parsley, and red pepper flakes to top of oiled dough.
10) Bake at 375°F for 25–30 minutes until top is lightly golden.
11) Let it rest for 10 minutes then drizzle with 1 TBS olive oil.
12) Remove bread from pan and place on cutting board and cut into rectangles.
13) Combine olive oil, balsamic vinegar, and grated Parmesan cheese in a small plate for dipping. Serve.

Dinner Rolls

Bread Base
(yields 6–7 rolls)

⅓ packet of active dry yeast (¼ oz packet)
¾ C warm water (110°F)
1 TBS white sugar plus ⅛ tsp white sugar
⅓ TBS salt
⅔ TBS canola oil
2¼ C bread flour, plus extra

Jalapeño–Cheddar Cheese
1 TBS jalapeño (chopped),
    plus extra sliced thin

⅓ C shredded sharp cheddar
    cheese, plus extra

Italian Herb and Cheese
1 TBS Italian herb seasoning
⅓ C shredded mozzarella cheese, plus extra

Roasted Garlic–Rosemary
1 large garlic bulb
1½ TBS fresh rosemary (removed from stems)
⅓ C shredded provolone cheese, plus extra

1) Bloom yeast in water with salt and canola oil in bowl.
2) Add flour and sugar to bowl of stand mixer and slowly mix together for 1 minute.
3) Add in ingredients for desired bread flavor. Mix together for 1 minute.
4) Add bloomed yeast mixture to bowl of stand mixer. Mix on medium speed for 1–2 minutes or until uniformed dough ball is formed.
5) Dust flat surface with flour. Remove bowl from stand mixer and turn dough onto floured surface and knead for 1–2 minutes.
6) Lightly coat a clean bowl with canola oil and place dough ball in bowl and cover with towel in room temperature for 1–1½ hours.
7) Dust flat surface with flour. Gently punch dough to expel air. Turn dough onto dusted surface and knead for 1 minute to form a uniform ball. Using a bench knife, split dough into 6–7 equal-size portions and roll into balls.
8) Lightly grease wells of a regular-sized muffin tin. Place dough balls into greased wells and cover with a towel and allow to rest for 1 hour.
9) Preheat oven to 375°F.
10) Uncover muffin tin and place in oven and bake for 30–35 minutes.
11) Remove from oven and place rolls on wire rack to cool.

Jalapeño–Cheddar Cheese
At the end of step 8, once dough balls are placed in wells of muffin tin, add a sprinkle of shredded sharp cheddar cheese to tops of dough and lay 2–3 slices of jalapeños on top of cheese.

Italian Herb and Cheese
At the end of step 8, once dough balls are placed in wells of muffin tin, add a sprinkle of shredded mozzarella cheese to tops of dough.

Roasted Garlic–Rosemary
For roasted garlic, preheat oven to 350°F. Next, slice garlic bulb in half and drizzle both halves with olive oil and season with sprinkle of salt and black pepper. Place the 2 halves together and wrap bulb in tin foil. Place on a baking sheet and bake for 40–45 minutes. Remove from oven and unwrap bulb, and allow to cool for 10–15 minutes.

At the end of step 8, once dough balls are placed in wells of muffin tin, add a sprinkle of shredded provolone cheese to tops of dough.

Brazilian Cheese Bread (Pão de Queijo)

Bread
(yields 24 rolls)

1 large egg
⅔ C whole milk
⅓ C olive oil

1½ C tapioca flour
¼ C grated Parmesan cheese
¼ C grated mozzarella cheese
1 tsp salt

1) Preheat oven to 350°F.
2) Add egg, milk, olive oil, tapioca flour, Parmesan cheese, mozzarella cheese, and salt to blender. Blend all ingredients together until smooth. You may have to blend a few times and scrape sides of blender to incorporate everything.
3) Using cooking spray, grease a 24-well mini muffin tin (or 2 12-well mini muffin tins). Pour mixture into wells, leaving about ⅛ inch from top.
4) Place in oven and bake for 20–25 minutes until bread has light golden brown color.
5) Remove from oven and allow to cool for 5 minutes. Transfer bread to bread basket or bowl and serve warm.

SALADS

Quinoa Salad

1½ C brown rice (cooked and cooled)
¾ C quinoa red and white mixture
   (cooked and cooled)
¾ C English cucumber (finely diced)
1 C kale (finely diced)
3 TBS cilantro leaves and stems (finely diced)
⅔ C mung beans (cooked and cooled)
⅔ C red bell pepper (finely diced)
⅔ C red lentils (cooked and cooled)

⅔ C Roma tomato (finely diced)
2 TBS lemon juice
¼ C olive oil
1½ TBS white vinegar
2 tsp water
1½ tsp ras el hanout seasoning
salt
black pepper

1) In a large bowl, combine cooked and cooled brown rice, quinoa, mung beans, and red lentils. Mix together. Next, add cucumber, kale, cilantro, red bell pepper, and tomato to bowl. Mix together.
2) In a separate bowl, combine lemon juice, olive oil, water, white vinegar, and ras el hanout seasoning. Mix together to combine.
3) Slowly add seasoning mixture to quinoa and mix together to incorporate.
4) Add salt and pepper to taste. If desired, add more ras el hanout seasoning for more spice.

Herb Goat Cheese and Candied Walnut Salad

Salad
4 oz of baby spinach
4 oz of spring mix arugula
3 oz of herb goat cheese
2 TBS sweet drop peppers
½ C croutons

Candied Walnuts
⅔ C walnuts (halved)
1 TBS honey
1 TBS maple syrup
1 TBS water

Dressing
1 TBS red wine vinegar
2 tsp whole grain Dijon mustard
3 TBS walnut oil
1 TBS honey
¼ tsp onion powder
¼ tsp salt
fresh cracked black pepper

Optional Toppings
red onion (cut into rings)

Dressing
1) In a small bowl, combine red wine vinegar, Dijon mustard, walnut oil, honey, onion powder, and salt. Mix together. Add desired amount of black pepper to taste. Set dressing aside.

Candied Walnuts
1) Place a nonstick pan over medium-low heat. Add walnuts to pan and toast for 3–4 minutes or until walnuts slightly begin to brown, occasionally turning. Lower heat to low.
2) In a small bowl, mix together honey, maple syrup, and water. Add mixture to walnuts. Toss together and cook for 1–2 minutes or until walnuts are coated.
3) Remove from heat and set aside to cool.

Salad
1) Wash and dry spinach and arugula.
2) Add spinach and arugula to salad bowl. Tear or cut chunks of herb goat cheese and add to salad mixture. Add drop peppers and croutons. Toss together.
3) Add candied walnuts to salad and toss together.
4) Add ⅔ of dressing to salad and toss together to coat salad.

Serving

Place salad in bowls and garnish with red onion rings (optional). If more dressing is desired, serve on the side to avoid making salad to wet.

White Bean and Kale Salad with Creamy Tahini Dressing

Kale Salad
10 oz kale (chopped, with
   large stems removed)
2 TBS fresh lemon juice
1 TBS olive oil
1 TBS maple syrup
1 clove garlic (minced)
salt
pepper

White Beans
1 15 oz can of white or butter
   beans (drained and rinsed)
1 TBS fresh lemon juice
1 TBS olive oil
¼ tsp salt
2 TBS fresh parsley (chopped)

Tahini Dressing
⅓ C tahini
1 clove garlic (minced)
3 TBS fresh lemon juice
2 TBS maple syrup
3 TBS hot water
salt

black pepper

Garlic Croutons—*Optional*
2 C French baguette (cut into ½–1 inch cubes)
¼ C olive oil
¼ tsp garlic powder
¼ tsp salt
¼ tsp black pepper
1½ tsp dried parsley

Sautéed Shrimp—*Optional*
1 LB medium-sized shrimp
   (deveined and cleaned)
1½ TBS olive oil
¼ tsp allspice
¼ tsp cumin
½ tsp garlic powder
½ tsp onion powder
¼ tsp cayenne pepper
¼ tsp ground ginger
¼ tsp salt
¼ tsp black pepper

Additional Ingredients
shaved Parmesan cheese

Kale Salad
1) Wash and rinse kale.
2) In small bowl, combine lemon juice, olive oil, maple syrup, and garlic. Whisk together and pour over kale. Using hands, toss together kale and mixture to coat kale. Set aside to marinate.

White Beans
1) Combine all ingredients in a bowl and toss together. Set aside for 5 minutes.

Tahini Dressing
1) In a bowl, combine tahini, garlic, lemon juice, and maple syrup. Whisk together. Add salt and pepper to taste.
2) Add 1 TBS of hot water at a time to dressing to thin it out and whisk together. If dressing is still too thick, add more water to desired consistency.
3) Set aside. Allow to set for 5 minutes.

Serving

When ready to serve, combine white beans, kale salad, and Parmesan cheese. Toss together. Next, add ⅔ of dressing to salad and toss together. Serve remaining dressing on the side. (Optional: when plating, add croutons and shrimp).

Optional Items

Garlic Croutons
1) Preheat oven to 350°F.
2) Place cut baguette cubes onto baking sheet. Drizzle with olive oil and add garlic powder, dried parsley, salt, and black pepper. Mix all items on baking sheet until evenly coated. Spread out croutons onto baking sheet.
3) Place in oven for 15–20 minutes or until croutons take on golden brown color. Remove from oven and allow to cool.

Sautéed Shrimp
1) Add cleaned shrimp to bowl and combine 1 TBS olive oil, allspice, cumin, garlic powder, onion powder, cayenne pepper, ground ginger, salt, and pepper. Toss together to coat shrimp.
2) Place pan on stove over medium heat and add ½ TBS olive oil to pan. Place shrimp into pan and cook on one side for 2 minutes then flip over and cook for another 1–2 minutes or until shrimp is no longer translucent (cook in batches if pan is not large enough). Remove from heat and allow to cool.

Caprese Herb Salad

Herb Salad
1 C cilantro leaves
1 C flat-leaf parsley
1 C dill sprigs
1 C basil leaves
2 C arugula
2 C butter lettuce
1½ C mozzarella pearls
1 C halved cherry tomatoes

2 TBS pomegranate seeds

Balsamic Vinaigrette
⅓ C balsamic vinegar
⅓ C olive oil
1½ TBS honey
1 TBS lemon juice
¼ tsp black pepper

Herb Salad
1) Wash and clean cilantro, parsley, basil, arugula, and butter lettuce. Once cleaned and dried, roughly chop cilantro, parsley, basil, dill sprigs, and butter lettuce. Add to large bowl with arugula.
2) Add mozzarella pearls, halved cherry tomatoes, and pomegranate seeds to bowl with lettuce and herbs. Mix together.

Balsamic Vinaigrette
1) In a small bowl, add balsamic vinegar, olive oil, honey, lemon juice, and black pepper. Whisk together until combined.

Plating

Add desired amount of salad to bowl or plate. Whisk vinaigrette together and then add to small dipping cup to serve dressing on the side. *Do not dress salad before serving.* Finish with additional cracked black pepper if desired.

SOUPS

Wonton Soup

Wontons
(yields 32 wontons)

⅓ LB ground chicken
⅓ LB fresh shrimp (finely chopped)
2 tsp soy sauce
2 tsp chives (chopped)
1 tsp rice wine vinegar
1 tsp cornstarch
1 tsp grated ginger
1 garlic clove (grated)
½ tsp crushed red pepper flakes
½ tsp sesame oil
1 package of square wonton wrappers
¼ C water

Soup Broth
6 C chicken broth
2" of fresh ginger
3 cloves of garlic (smashed)
2 tsp soy sauce
¼ tsp sesame oil
4 baby bok choy (sliced in half)
1 C shiitake mushrooms (sliced)

Additional Toppings
scallions (thinly sliced)
sriracha hot sauce

Wontons
1) In a large bowl, combine ground chicken and chopped shrimp and mix together. Next, add soy sauce, chives, cornstarch, rice wine vinegar, ginger, garlic, red pepper flakes, and sesame oil. Mix together until combined.
2) Fill mixture into a piping bag.
3) Remove wonton wrappers from package and separate. Place one wrapper on flat surface and pipe in ½ tsp of mixture into center of wonton wrapper. Using fingers, rub water on two sides of wrapper and fold over wonton wrapper to make a triangle. Press firmly together to seal mixture inside. Next, wet one corner of wonton and fold over to other side to form a circle and press together to seal. Set aside and repeat.

Soup Broth
1) Add chicken broth, soy sauce, and sesame oil to large pot over medium-high heat.
2) Peel fresh ginger to remove outer skin. Cut ginger into slices. Add sliced ginger and garlic to pot. Heat for 5–6 minutes.
3) Add mushrooms and bok choy to pot and heat for 3–4 minutes.
4) When broth begins to boil, reduce heat to medium-low and simmer.
5) Add 15–20 wontons to broth and cook for 2–3 minutes or until wonton is cooked through.
6) Remove from heat and serve.

Note: You can freeze remaining wontons to use another time.

Curried Butternut Squash Soup

Soup
1 TBS avocado oil
2 medium shallots (thinly sliced)
2 large garlic cloves (minced)
6 C peeled and chopped butternut squash
1½ TBS of curry powder
¼ tsp ground cinnamon
⅛ tsp ground nutmeg
16 oz light coconut milk
2 C vegetable stock
2 TBS maple syrup

1 TBS chili paste
salt
black pepper

Optional Toppings
crumbled bacon
pepitas (toasted pumpkin seeds)
additional coconut milk
additional chili paste
parsley

1) In a large pot over medium heat, add avocado oil, shallots, and garlic and sauté until shallots are translucent (approx. 1–2 minutes). Stir continuously.
2) Add butternut squash and season with pinch of salt, pinch of black pepper, curry powder, cinnamon, and nutmeg. Stir to coat. Cook for 4 minutes, stirring occasionally.
3) Add coconut milk, vegetable stock, maple syrup, and chili paste. Stir together and then cover pot.
4) Bring to a low boil over medium heat and then reduce to a low heat and simmer for 15 minutes or until butternut squash is fork-tender.
5) Using an immersion blender, puree on high until creamy and smooth. If you do not have an immersion blender, using a large ladle, transfer to blender and puree on high until smooth and return to pot.
6) Taste and add more salt and/or pepper if desired. Cook for an additional 3–4 minutes over medium heat, stirring occasionally.
7) Serve.

Chicken Wild Rice Soup

Wild Rice Soup
¾ C uncooked wild rice blend
1¼ LB boneless-skinless chicken
    breast (cut into ½ inch cubes)
1 medium yellow onion (chopped)
2 large carrots (diced)
3 ribs celery (diced)
8 oz white mushroom (sliced)
8 TBS butter
2 tsp minced garlic
4½ C chicken broth
1¼ tsp fresh thyme

1¼ tsp fresh marjoram
1¼ tsp fresh sage
1¼ tsp fresh rosemary
½ C all-purpose flour
1½ C milk
½ C heavy cream
½ tsp lemon zest

Additional Toppings
crunchy fried onions
thinly sliced scallions

1) Prepare wild rice as directed by package.
2) Once rice has been cooking for 10 minutes, add 2 TBS of butter to a large pot over medium heat and add carrots, onions, celery, and mushrooms. Sauté for 4 minutes or until onions become translucent. Next, add garlic and sauté for 1 minute.
3) Add chicken broth, thyme, rosemary, marjoram, and sage to pot. Increase heat to medium-high and add chicken and bring to a boil. Season with salt and black pepper to taste. Once pot begins to boil, cover pot with lid and reduce heat to medium-low and allow to cook for 15 minutes.
4) In a separate medium-sized saucepan, melt 6 TBS of butter over medium-low heat. Add flour to pan and cook for 1–1½ minutes, whisking constantly.
5) While whisking constantly, slowly pour in milk to pan with rue. Once milk is fully incorporated, whisk in heavy cream. Cook mixture and stir constantly until mixture thickens.
6) Remove large pot from heat. Add milk mixture to large pot and mix in. Next, add cooked wild rice and lemon zest to large pot and mix together.
7) Allow soup to cool and serve. Garnish soup as desired for serving.

Vegetarian Alternative
If you wish to make the wild rice soup vegetarian, you can omit chicken
and replace chicken broth with vegetable broth.

Thai Curry Soup

2 TBS olive oil
3 large cloves garlic (minced)
2½ TBS lemongrass (minced)
2 tsp grated ginger
3 tsp red curry paste
1 TBS chili-garlic paste
1 32 oz carton chicken broth
20 oz lite coconut milk
1 TBS soy sauce
1 TBS white sugar
2 TBS fresh lime juice
½ C chopped cilantro, plus extra

1 tsp chopped Thai basil
1 C sliced shiitake mushrooms
   (stems removed)
3 mini red sweet peppers (seeded and sliced)
2 scallions (thinly sliced)
12 medium raw shrimp (peeled and deveined)

Additional Ingredients
2–3 C of cooked jasmine rice or 2–4
   oz of cooked rice noodles
lime wedges
chopped cilantro

1) Place stockpot on stove over medium-high heat and add olive oil. Heat for 1 minute.
2) Add garlic, lemongrass, and ginger; cook and stir until aromatic for about 1 minute. Add red curry paste and cook and stir for 30 seconds.
3) Add half carton of chicken broth to pot and stir until red curry paste has dissolved. Once dissolved, add remaining half of carton to pot with soy sauce and sugar and stir together. Bring pot to boil then reduce to medium-low heat, cover pot, and simmer for 20 minutes.
4) Next, stir in coconut milk, mushrooms, mini sweet peppers, lime juice, chili-garlic paste, Thai basil, and cilantro. Increase heat to medium-high and cook for 5–6 minutes.
5) Add shrimp to pot and cook for 3–4 minutes or until shrimp are no longer translucent. Remove from heat. Add one thinly sliced scallion to pot and stir together.

Serving
Place 1 C of cooked rice or 2 oz of cooked rice noodles to bowl. Stir pot and, using ladle, ladle about 1–1½ C of soup into bowl. Place 4 shrimp on top of soup in bowl and garnish with thinly sliced scallions, chopped cilantro, and/or lime wedge.

Vegetarian Alternative
Replace chicken broth with vegetable broth and omit shrimp. In place of shrimp, add ¼ cup of sliced carrots and ½ cup of button mushrooms.

SIDES

Potatoes Gratin

3–4 medium-sized Yukon Gold potatoes
2 TBS butter
1 TBS all-purpose flour
3 cloves garlic (minced)
1 C milk

1 tsp salt
¼ tsp black pepper
¼ C shredded cheddar cheese
2 TBS shredded Parmesan cheese

1) Preheat oven to 350°F.
2) In a small pot, melt butter over medium-low heat. Add garlic to pot and cook for 1–2 minutes or until aromatic. Add flour, salt, and black pepper to pot and whisk together until no lumps remain.
3) While continuously whisking, slowly add milk to mixture. Whisk until smooth. Add cheddar cheese to mixture and whisk until smooth.
4) Bring mixture to a boil, cook for 2–3 minutes, then remove from heat.
5) Peel potatoes and cut them into ⅛ inch thick slices. Place sliced potatoes into small baking dish and fan out (this should form two rows along sides of dish).
6) Pour cream sauce over top of potatoes then sprinkle with Parmesan cheese.
7) Place dish in the oven and bake for 1 hour or until top is golden brown and bubbly.
8) Remove dish from oven and allow to cool for 5–10 minutes.
9) Serve warm.

Sweet-and-Spicy Cauliflower

Cauliflower
1 large head of cauliflower
cooking spray
1 tsp garlic salt
salt
black pepper
2 TBS scallions (sliced thinly)
1 TBS sesame seeds

Sweet-and-Spicy Sauce
¼ C honey
¼ C soy sauce
1 TBS sriracha hot sauce
1 TBS hoisin sauce
3 cloves garlic (minced)
2 TBS cornstarch

Cauliflower
1) Preheat oven to 400°F.
2) Cut cauliflower into bite-size florets and lay out on baking sheet.
3) Spray florets with cooking spray. Sprinkle garlic salt over florets and season with salt and pepper to taste. Using hands, toss together florets to coat florets with cooking spray and seasoning.
4) Place baking sheet in oven and cook for 15–20 minutes. Remove baking sheet from oven before florets begin to lightly brown.
5) Allow florets to cool for 5–10 minutes.
6) Place florets in a bowl, add scallions and pour sauce into bowl, and gently toss together.
7) Place cauliflower florets in serving dish and top with sesame seeds.

Sweet-and-Spicy Sauce
1) Once cauliflower has been in the oven for 10 minutes, place small saucepan on stove over medium heat.
2) Add honey, soy sauce, sriracha, hoisin sauce, and garlic to pan and cook for 4–5 minutes.
3) Next, add cornstarch and whisk it into mixture until no lumps remain. Bring mixture to a boil and remove from heat.
4) Allow sauce to cool and thicken before adding to cauliflower.
Note: Sweet-and-spicy sauce makes for a great dipping sauce for chicken, pork, or shrimp.

Roasted Garlic Mashed Potatoes

1 LB Yukon Gold potatoes
2½ TBS butter
2 TBS cream cheese
2½ TBS buttermilk
1 small head of garlic

⅛ tsp garlic powder
salt
black pepper
olive oil
1 scallion (thinly sliced)

Roasted Garlic
1) Preheat oven to 375°F.
2) Slice head of garlic in half horizontally. Drizzle both halves with olive oil and season with salt and pepper.
3) Place two halves together and wrap garlic in tin foil and place on baking sheet. Place in oven and cook for 1 hour.
4) Remove from oven and allow to cool. Once cool to touch, remove garlic clove halves from skin and set aside.

Mashed Potatoes
1) Place a medium-sized pot on stove with salted water over high heat.
2) Peel 1 LB of Yukon Gold potatoes and wash. Slice peeled potatoes into 1–1½ inch sections. Add sliced potatoes to pot with salted water. Allow to boil until potatoes are fork-tender.
3) Remove potatoes from water and add to large bowl.
4) Add roasted garlic cloves, butter, cream cheese, buttermilk, and garlic powder to bowl. Using a whisk, mash and mix together items in bowl. Once potatoes take on smooth consistency, add salt and pepper to taste.
5) Garnish mashed potatoes with thinly sliced scallions.

Sautéed Green Beans

12 oz fresh whole green beans
5 oz small cherry tomatoes
1 medium shallot (thinly sliced)
3 cloves garlic (thinly sliced)
2 dried red chilies
2 TBS olive oil

1 TBS sesame oil
1 TBS chili oil
1 TBS teriyaki sauce
⅛ tsp salt
⅛ tsp black pepper

1) Using steam pot, steam green beans for 4–5 minutes.
2) Remove green beans from steamer and place in bowl of ice water to stop cooking process.
3) Heat 1 TBS of olive oil, sesame oil, and chili oil in a pan. Add shallots, garlic, and chilies. Cook for 1 minute.
4) Add tomatoes to pan and cook for 2 minutes.
5) Add green beans to pan and cook for 5 minutes.
6) Add 1 TBS olive oil, salt, black pepper, and teriyaki sauce to pan and toss together.
7) Remove from heat and serve.

Creamed Spinach

15 oz baby spinach
2 TBS butter
1 small onion (finely chopped)
3 cloves garlic (minced)
½ C milk
¼ C heavy cream

4 oz cream cheese
⅓ C shredded Parmesan cheese, plus extra
pinch of cayenne pepper
pinch of nutmeg
salt
black pepper

1) Add butter to pan and place over medium-low heat. Add onions and garlic to pan and cook for 2–3 minutes or until onions are softened.
2) Add spinach to pan and cook for 4–5 minutes or until spinach is wilted. Stir occasionally.
3) Add milk, heavy cream, and cream cheese to pan and cook for 4–5 minutes. Stir continuously to incorporate all ingredients.
4) Season with cayenne pepper and nutmeg. Stir into cream sauce. Next, season with salt and pepper to taste.
5) Remove pan from heat and add Parmesan cheese to pan. Stir cheese into cream sauce.
6) Transfer creamed spinach to serving dish and top with sprinkle of Parmesan cheese.
7) Serve warm.

ENTRÉES

Chicken with Mushroom-Spinach Cream Sauce

4 large boneless-skinless chicken
  breast (about 2 LB)
4 TBS butter
salt
black pepper
8 oz white mushrooms (sliced)

3 C baby spinach leaves
1½ tsp minced garlic
1 TBS all-purpose flour
⅓ C white wine
¾ C heavy cream
¼ C shredded Parmesan cheese

1) Wash and dry chicken breasts. Generously season chicken breasts with salt and black pepper.
2) Place a large pan on stove over medium heat. Melt 2 TBS of butter.
3) Preheat oven to 300°F.
4) Add chicken breasts to pan and cook for 4–5 minutes on each side or until golden brown and cooked through.
5) Remove chicken from pan and place on a baking sheet and put in oven to keep warm.
6) Add 1 TBS of butter to pan and add mushrooms. Cook for 4–5 minutes or until tender. Remove mushrooms from pan and set aside in a bowl. Wipe pan clean with damp paper towel.
7) Add 1 TBS butter and garlic to pan over medium-low heat. While whisking constantly, sprinkle in flour and whisk together for 1 minute.
8) Add white wine to pan and whisk together with butter-flour mixture. Cook for 2–3 minutes.
9) Add heavy cream to pan and cook for 3–4 minutes or until mixture thickens. Stir in Parmesan cheese and add salt and black pepper to taste.
10) Add spinach and mushrooms to cream mixture and mix. Cook for 2 minutes.
11) Remove chicken breast from oven and add to pan. Nestle the chicken breast into cream sauce and cook for 2–3 minutes.
12) Remove from heat and allow to slightly cool. Serve.

Serving

Serve dish with wild rice or buttered noodles. Place 1 cup of cooked wild rice or noodles on plate and add chicken breast. Spoon sauce over chicken. Serve.

Garlic Chicken-Shrimp Fried Rice

5 C cooked rice
8 oz boneless-skinless chicken breast
4 oz medium-sized shrimp
½ medium yellow onion (diced)
2 large garlic cloves (sliced)
1–2 dried chilies
1 mini red sweet pepper (seeded and diced)
1 mini yellow sweet pepper (seeded and diced)
1 mini orange sweet pepper
   (seeded and diced)
½ TBS garlic-chili paste
1 large egg
½ C butter

3 tsp soy sauce
1 TBS corn oil
¾ TBS sesame oil
¾ TBS chili oil
½ tsp seasoning salt
½ TBS garlic powder, plus extra
½ tsp ground ginger, plus extra
½ tsp onion powder, plus extra
1/16 tsp cayenne pepper
¼ tsp ground white pepper
3 scallions (sliced), plus extra
   for garnish (optional)

1) Prepare rice as directed by package. It is best to use rice that was made the day before.
2) Using cooking mallet, pound chicken breast until ¼ inch thick and cut into ½ inch cubes. Next, chop shrimp into ¼ inch pieces and place in a bowl.
3) Season chicken and shrimp with seasoning salt, cayenne pepper, white pepper, $\frac{1}{16}$ tsp garlic powder, and $\frac{1}{16}$ tsp ground ginger.
4) Place ½ TBS corn oil, ½ TBS sesame oil, and ½ TBS chili oil in wok over medium-high heat. Allow oils to heat for 1 minute. Add chicken and shrimp to wok and cook for 4–5 minutes, stirring occasionally. Remove chicken and shrimp from wok and set aside.
5) Place ½ TBS corn oil in wok over medium-high heat. Allow oil to heat for 1 minute. Add garlic, onion, dried chili(s), and sweet peppers to corn oil and cook for 1–2 minutes or until onions are translucent.
6) Add cooked rice and butter to wok and mix together. Cook for 4 minutes, stirring occasionally and tossing together.
7) Add chicken and shrimp to wok and toss with rice. Next, add garlic-chili paste, soy sauce, ½ tsp garlic powder, ½ tsp ground ginger, and ½ tsp onion powder to wok and mix together. Cook for 3–4 minutes.
8) Form a well in the middle of wok and crack a large egg in center of well. Stirring continuously, scramble egg. Once egg is scrambled, mix together with fried rice.
9) Allow to cook for 2 minutes and then remove wok from heat.
10) Add scallions to fried rice and toss together to incorporate.
11) Serve.

Vegetarian Alternative
If you desire to make vegetarian fried rice, omit chicken, shrimp, and egg. In place, use additional ½ of medium yellow onion and 1 additional red, yellow, and orange sweet peppers.

Cedar Plank–Grilled Teriyaki Glazed Salmon and Garlic-Butter Cauliflower Fried Rice

Teriyaki Marinade
1 C water
¼ C soy sauce
5 tsp packed brown sugar
2 TBS honey
½ tsp ground ginger
¼ tsp garlic powder
¼ tsp onion powder
2 TBS cornstarch
¼ cold water
2–4 oz fillets of salmon
1 thin cedar plank

Cauliflower Fried Rice
1½ TBS olive oil

2 cloves garlic (thinly sliced)
1 TBS shallots (thinly sliced)
2 small dried chilies
2–10 oz bags of frozen
    cauliflower rice (thawed)
1 tsp garlic powder
½ tsp onion powder
¼ tsp cayenne pepper
¼ tsp paprika
¼ tsp ground ginger
1 large egg (optional)
1½ TBS soy sauce
½ TBS sesame oil
2 TBS butter
2–3 scallions (finely sliced)

Teriyaki Salmon
1) Combine 1 cup of water, soy sauce, brown sugar, honey, ground ginger, garlic powder, and onion powder in saucepan over medium heat. Cook until nearly heated through, for about 1–2 minutes.
2) Combine cornstarch and ¼ cup of cold water and mix together in a cup until cornstarch is dissolved. Add slurry to saucepan with heated ingredients. Cook and stir sauce until thickened, for about 5–8 minutes. Remove saucepan from heat and allow to cool.
3) Place salmon fillets in shallow container with lid. Once teriyaki mixture has cooled, pour it over salmon fillets and coat fillets. Cover container and place in refrigerator for 1–2 hours to marinate.
4) Soak cedar plank in water for 1–2 hours.
5) After salmon has marinated, heat grill to 400°F and place cedar plank on grill.
6) Once grill is heated, add salmon fillets to cedar plank and allow to cook for about 20 minutes. Save marinate.
7) After 20 minutes of cooking, use reserved marinate and brush it onto the salmon fillets. Allow to cook for another 5 minutes and brush again with marinate. Cook for an additional 5 minutes.
8) After 30 minutes, remove salmon from grill and allow to rest.

Cauliflower Fried Rice
1) Add olive oil to wok over medium heat, with garlic, shallots, and dried chilies. Sauté for about 2–3 minutes.
2) Add thawed cauliflower rice to wok and toss to coat with oil. Cover wok and allow to cook for 5–7 minutes, lightly stirring occasionally. Be sure not to mash cauliflower.
3) Add garlic powder, onion powder, cayenne pepper, paprika, and ground ginger and toss with cauliflower. Allow to cook for 5–7 minutes, stirring occasionally; you want to start to form a light crust on the bottom layer of cauliflower rice.
4) If you choose to add egg, crack egg in a small bowl and lightly whisk with fork until yolk and whites are combined. Form a medium-sized hole in the middle of cauliflower and pour egg mixture into wok. Stir egg mixture until cooked and combine with cauliflower rice.

5) Next, add soy sauce, sesame oil, and butter to cauliflower and mix together. Allow to cook for 5–7 minutes, lightly stirring occasionally.

6) Remove wok from heat and add salt to taste.

7) Add chopped scallions to cauliflower fried rice and give it a light toss.

Plating

Add 1–1½ cups of cauliflower rice to center of plate to form a bed of rice. Using a pair of tongs, gently place salmon fillet on top of the bed of cauliflower rice. Garnish with scallions.

Peruvian Lomo Saltado

Lomo Saltado
4 TBS vegetable oil
1 LB sirloin steak (cut into ½ inch strips)
½ medium red onion (sliced)
2 Roma tomatoes (sliced)
3 cloves garlic (minced)
1 medium green bell pepper (sliced)
1 medium red bell pepper (sliced)
1 medium yellow bell pepper (sliced)
1 medium orange bell pepper (sliced)
1 TBS chili paste
4 TBS soy sauce

3 TBS white vinegar
2 TBS cilantro (chopped)
salt
black pepper

Additional Items
1 LB french fries (cooked)
1½ C cooked white rice
extra chopped cilantro

Lomo Saltado
1) Heat 2 TBS of vegetable oil in large pan over medium-high heat. Add sirloin steak and lightly season with salt and black pepper. Cook until browned for about 4–5 minutes. Remove from pan.
2) Heat 2 TBS of vegetable oil in same pan over medium heat and add garlic and onions. Cook for about 4 minutes until lightly brown. Add tomatoes, bell peppers, and chili paste and cook for 5 minutes.
3) Add cooked steak back to pan. Add soy sauce, white vinegar, and cilantro to pan and toss together. Cook for 1–2 minutes.

Plating
Serve with cooked rice and cooked French fries. Garnish with chopped cilantro (optional).

Pan-Seared Walleye with Brown Butter Lemon Sauce and Cashew-Green Beans

Walleye
2 6 oz walleye fillets
salt
black pepper
2 tsp olive oil

Green Beans
12 oz fresh green beans (blanched)
¼ C halved cashews
1½ TBS walnut oil
salt
black pepper

Brown Butter Lemon Sauce
5 TBS butter

4 cloves garlic (smashed)
¼ C white wine
1 TBS fresh lemon juice
3 TBS capers
1 TBS parsley (chopped)
1 tsp thyme (chopped)
black pepper

Garnish
fresh dill sprigs
lemon wedges

Walleye
1) Lightly drizzle ½ tsp of olive oil on each side of walleye fillet and coat fillet. Season each side of walleye fillet with salt and black pepper.
2) Heat skillet over medium-low heat. Once skillet is warm, place fillet in skillet and cook for 2 minutes. Turn fillet and cook next side for 2 minutes or until lightly browned.
3) Remove from heat.

Green Beans
1) Place steamer pot on stove over high heat and boil 2–3 cups of water. Once water is boiling, place green beans into steamer basket and cover to steam for 2–3 minutes. Remove green beans and place in bowl with ice water to stop cooking. Leave in ice water for 1 minute.
2) In pan over medium heat, add cashews to lightly toast for 2–3 minutes.
3) Add walnut oil and green beans to pan and toss together until sautéed for 2 minutes. Season with salt and black pepper.
4) Remove from heat.

Brown Butter Lemon Sauce
1) Place saucepan on medium heat and add butter. Cook butter, stirring occasionally, until butter takes on brown color. This should take about 3–4 minutes.
2) Once butter is browned, lower heat to low and add garlic cloves, white wine, parsley, and thyme. Toss together and heat for 1 minute. Remove from heat and set aside to steep for 2 minutes.
3) Pour sauce through fine metal strainer into a bowl.
4) Add capers and lemon juice to butter sauce. Season with black pepper.

Serving
Place bed of green beans and cashews on plate. Using a fish spatula, lay walleye fillet over green beans. Using a tablespoon, drizzle desired amount of sauce over walleye and green beans. Garnish with sprig of fresh dill and lemon wedge.

Miso Glazed Chilean Sea Bass and Napa Cabbage Slaw

Miso Glazed Sea Bass
⅓ C sake
⅓ C mirin
2 TBS soy sauce
½ C honey
⅓ C miso paste
2 TBS chopped scallions
4 (4 oz) Chilean sea bass fillets

Napa Cabbage Slaw
½ Napa cabbage (thinly sliced)
½ C scallions (thinly sliced)
¼ fresh mint (minced)
¼ cilantro (roughly chopped)

Sesame Ginger Vinaigrette
1½ TBS rice wine vinegar
1 TBS soy sauce
1 TBS sesame oil
½ TBS honey
¾ TBS grated ginger
¼ TBS chili paste (optional)

Sea Bass
1) In a medium-sized container, mix sake, mirin, soy sauce, ¼ cup of honey, miso paste, and scallions.
2) Add sea bass fillets to marinate. Cover and place in refrigerator for 2–3 hours.
3) Remove sea bass fillets from marinate and place on a large parchment paper–lined baking sheet. *(Do not discard marinate.)*
4) Turn broiler to *high* in oven. Raise top rack in oven to top level (6 inches from top).
5) Place fillets on top rack and allow to broil for 5–7 minutes.
6) Remove fillets from oven.

Miso Glaze
1) In a small saucepan, add reserved marinate and ¼ cup honey.
2) Place saucepan on stove top over medium-high heat and cook down marinate until reduced to half (5–10 minutes).
3) Remove glaze from heat and allow to cool.
4) Using a brush, brush glaze onto sea bass fillets to desired amount.

Napa Cabbage Slaw
1) In large bowl, combine Napa cabbage, scallions, mint, and cilantro.
2) In a separate bowl, combine rice wine vinegar, soy sauce, sesame oil, honey, and ginger (and chili paste).
3) Pour vinaigrette over slaw and mix together.

Plating

Place ring mold on serving plate and lightly fill ring mold with slaw. *Do not firmly compact the slaw into the ring mold.* Once filled to desired level, lift ring mold off plate slowly. Place sea bass fillet on plate next to cabbage slaw. Add an additional dollop of miso glaze to plate.

Braised Beef Short Ribs and Herb Polenta

Braised Short Ribs
2½ LB of beef short ribs (about 4 short ribs)
salt
black pepper
3 TBS canola oil
1½ C pearl onions (left whole)
1 C baby carrots
1 stock celery (chopped)
2½ TBS all-purpose flour
1 TBS tomato paste
2½ C dry red wine (preferably Cabernet
    Sauvignon or Pinot Noir)
8 sprigs flat-leaf parsley
5 sprigs thyme
4 sprigs oregano
2 sprigs rosemary

3 dried bay leaves
6 large cloves garlic (smashed)
3 C beef stock

Polenta
4 C beef stock (or vegetable stock)
1¼ tsp salt
1¼ C yellow cornmeal
½ C grated Parmesan
½ C whole milk
4 TBS butter
1 tsp dried parsley
1 tsp dried thyme
1 tsp dried oregano
¼ tsp ground black pepper

Short Ribs
1) Preheat oven to 350°F.
2) Generously season short ribs with salt and black pepper on all sides.
3) Place Dutch oven on stove over medium-high heat. Add canola oil and heat for 3-4 minutes.
4) Place short ribs in Dutch oven and brown short ribs on all sides (about 1½–2 minutes per side).
5) Remove short ribs and transfer to plate.
6) Add onions, carrots, and celery to pot and cook over medium-high heat for 5 minutes or until onions begin to brown. Be sure to stir often.
7) Next, add flour and tomato paste to pot and cook for 2–3 minutes. Stir constantly to coat all vegetables.
8) Add red wine to pot and stir together. Add short ribs and drippings from plate back to the pot. Bring to a boil then reduce heat to medium and simmer for 25 minutes.
9) Tie herbs together with cooking twine into a bouquet and add to pot, along with beef stock and garlic. Mix together and bring pot to boil for 5 minutes. Turn off heat and cover pot.
10) Transfer covered pot to oven and cook for 2½ hours.
11) Remove pot from oven and gently transfer short ribs to platter. Discard herbs. Use a spoon and remove excess fat from top of sauce and discard. Season sauce with salt and black pepper.

Polenta
1) In a large saucepan, bring beef stock to boil with salt.
2) Gradually whisk in cornmeal while whisking constantly to ensure cornmeal is fully incorporated and no lumps remain.
3) Reduce heat to low and cook until mixture thickens and cornmeal is tender while stirring often (about 15 minutes).
4) Remove pan from heat and stir in cheese, milk, butter, parsley, thyme, oregano, and black pepper. Stir until butter and cheese are melted.

Plating
Using a ladle, add polenta to a shallow bowl and smooth out polenta. Using a pair of tongs, gently place short rib in the center of bowl and nestle into polenta. Use ladle and pour desired amount of sauce from pot over short rib and polenta (about ½ ladle full). Add pearl onions and carrots to bowl as well. Garnish with some green sprouts for a touch of color.

Chicken-Shrimp Pad Thai

Pad Thai
8 oz pad Thai noodles
4 TBS sesame oil
2 TBS chili oil
2 large eggs
1 6 oz chicken breast (diced
  into ½–1 inch pieces)
6 oz peeled and deveined
  medium-sized shrimp
⅓ C shallots (diced)
2 garlic cloves (minced)
½ C crushed dried peanuts
⅓ C scallions (diced)
¼ C cilantro (chopped)
1 C bean sprouts
salt
black pepper
⅛ tsp cayenne pepper
⅛ tsp garlic powder
⅛ tsp onion powder
⅛ tsp ground ginger
⅛ tsp ground mustard

Pad Thai Sauce
(yields 1 C)

3 TBS fish sauce
3 TBS rice vinegar
3 TBS light soy sauce
3 TBS light brown sugar
3 TBS driracha
2½ TBS lime juice
1½ TBS peanut butter

Additional Toppings
extra crushed peanuts
extra cilantro
extra bean sprouts
extra scallions
sliced jalapeño peppers
lime wedges

Pad Thai
  1) Prepare noodles as directed by packaging instructions. Once prepared, combine with 1 TBS sesame oil and set aside.
  2) Add 1 TBS of sesame oil to wok over medium heat. Lightly whisk eggs together and pour into wok with heated sesame oil. Cook until scrambled (about 1 minute). Remove from wok and set aside.
  3) In a bowl, combine chicken, shrimp, cayenne pepper, garlic powder, onion powder, ground ginger, ground mustard, pinch of salt, and pinch of black pepper.
  4) Add 2 TBS of sesame oil and chili oil over medium heat. Add shallots and garlic to wok and cook for 1 minute while stirring. Next, add seasoned chicken and shrimp to wok and cook until chicken is no longer pink in center. Remove wok from heat.
  5) Add eggs, bean sprouts, scallions, peanuts, cilantro, and noodles to wok and combine with chicken and shrimp.
  6) Add ¾ cup of pad Thai sauce to wok and combine together.
  7) Plate and garnish as desired.

Pad Thai Sauce
  1) Combine all ingredients together in a bowl and whisk together.

Saffron Three-Mushroom Risotto
with Seared Scallops

Saffron Risotto
6 C chicken stock
4 TBS olive oil
½ LB portobello mushrooms
½ LB white mushrooms
½ LB shiitake mushrooms
3 TBS shallots (diced)
1 TBS fresh garlic (diced)
1½ C Arborio rice
½ C dry white wine
4 TBS butter

3 TBS chives
⅓ C of grated Parmesan cheese
saffron
salt
black pepper

Seared Scallops
8 large sea scallops
2 TBS butter
salt
black pepper

Risotto
1) In a stockpot, add chicken stock and saffron and heat with low-medium heat (*do not boil*).
2) In a pan over medium heat, add 2 TBS olive oil, 1 TBS shallot, and garlic and sauté for 1 minute. Next, add portobello mushrooms, white mushroom, and shiitake mushrooms and cook until mushrooms are softened (approx. 5–7 minutes). Remove mushrooms from pan and set aside.
3) In a pan over medium heat, add 2 TBS olive oil and 2 TBS shallot and sauté for 1–2 minutes. Next, add Arborio rice to pan and coat with olive oil and stir for 1–2 minutes. Once rice is coated, add white wine. Stir together until white wine is fully absorbed.
4) Remove saffron threads from chicken stock and discard.
5) Add chicken stock to rice pan ½ cup at a time. Stir rice until liquid is absorbed. Continue adding liquid to rice and stirring continuously until rice is al dente (approx. 15–20 minutes).
6) Remove pan from heat and add in mushrooms, butter, Parmesan cheese, and chives. Gently incorporate ingredients as to not mash the rice. Add salt and black pepper to taste.

Seared Scallops
1) Lightly rinse off scallops and place on paper towel and gently pat each side dry.
2) In a skillet, heat butter over high heat.
3) Season scallops on both sides with salt and black pepper to taste.
4) Place scallops in hot skillet and sear for 1½ minutes per side. Scallops should have ¼ inch golden crust on each side and remain translucent in the center.

Vegetarian Alternative
Replace chicken stock with vegetable stock and omit scallops.

Sausage and Herb Ravioli with Champagne-Cream Sauce

Sausage Ravioli
(yields 18–20 ravioli)

4 sheets of fresh pasta ⅛ inch thick
½ LB ground sweet sausage
½ TBS minced garlic
1 TBS minced shallot
1 TBS fresh sage (finely chopped)
3 TBS fresh basil (finely chopped)
¼ tsp mustard powder
¼ tsp cayenne pepper
¼ tsp smoked paprika
1 tsp dried parsley
½ TBS olive oil
2 oz baby spinach
6 oz ricotta cheese
½ C shredded mozzarella cheese
salt
black pepper

Champagne-Cream Sauce
1½ TBS minced garlic
1½ TBS minced shallot
2 TBS olive oil
4 TBS butter
2 TBS fresh sage (finely chopped)
2 C dry champagne
2 C heavy cream
2 C grated parmigiana-Reggiano
salt
black pepper

Additional Toppings
extra basil
extra grated parmigiana-Reggiano
Ravioli

1) Place saucepan on stove over medium heat. Allow to warm for 1 minute.
2) Add garlic and shallot to pan and cook for 1 minute. Next, add sausage, sage, and 1 TBS basil to pan and stir together. Cook for 5 minutes.
3) Lower heat to medium-low. Add mustard powder, cayenne pepper, smoked paprika, and parsley to pan. Stir together and cook for 2 minutes. Add salt and pepper to taste. Remove mixture from pan and place in a bowl to cool.
4) Return saucepan to stove and place over medium-low heat. Add olive oil to pan with spinach and 2 TBS basil. Cook for 4–5 minutes until spinach is wilted.
5) Remove from heat and allow to cool.
6) Place a stockpot on the stove over high heat with salted water. Bring to boil.
7) In a large bowl, add ricotta, mozzarella cheese, cooled meat mixture, and cooled spinach. Stir together to combine. Add salt and pepper to taste.
8) Lay out 2 sheets of pasta on a floured bench top. Using ravioli stamps, lightly score each sheet to create ravioli spaces.
9) Add 1 TBS of ravioli filling to center of each prescored ravioli space.
10) Next, place remaining 2 pasta sheets on top of the pasta sheets with filling. Be sure to line up edges.
11) Using ravioli stamp, press down on sheets and ensure filling remains in the middle of ravioli. Be sure to press firmly to create a tight seal of dough.
12) Place stamped out ravioli onto a floured baking sheet.
13) Place prepared ravioli into stockpot with boiling water. Add 5–6 at a time. Allow ravioli to cook until they float to the top. Then use a slotted spoon and remove them from water and place into a serving plate or bowl.

Champagne-Cream Sauce
1) Place a saucepan with olive oil on stove over medium heat. Allow oil to warm for 1 minute.
2) Add garlic, shallot, and sage to pan and cook for 2 minutes. Stir occasionally.
3) Next, add butter to pan and allow to melt and stir together. Once butter is melted and incorporated, add champagne to pan. Cook until champagne is reduced by half.
4) Add heavy cream and stir together. Bring to a low boil for 1 minute.
5) Remove pan from heat and add parmigiana-Reggiano to pan and stir together.
6) Add salt and pepper to taste. Allow to cool for 5–10 minutes before serving. Stir occasionally.

Plating

Add six cooked ravioli to a plate or bowl. Using a ladle, add desired amount of sauce to the top of ravioli. Finish with a few sprinkles of chiffonade basil, grated parmigiana-Reggiano, and cracked black pepper.

Vegetarian Alternative

To make vegetarian ravioli, omit ground sausage and replace with an additional amount of 5 oz ricotta cheese, 2 oz baby spinach, 1 TBS fresh basil, ½ TBS fresh sage, ¼ C mozzarella cheese, and 1 large egg. Add these ingredients to step 7. For step 2, cook garlic, shallot, sage, and 1 TBS basil together for 2 minutes. Omit step 3 and add those ingredients to step 7.

Ratatouille

5 medium-sized Roma tomatoes
3 medium-sized yellow squash
3 medium-sized zucchini
3 medium-sized eggplant
½ medium-sized onion (chopped)
3 cloves garlic (chopped)
3 oz tomato paste
6 oz canned diced tomato
1½ C vegetable stock
3 TBS olive oil

1 TBS fresh basil
½ TBS fresh oregano
¼ Fresh thyme
½ tsp salt + ¼ tsp salt
¼ tsp black pepper + ¼ tsp of black pepper
¼ tsp white pepper
½ TBS garlic powder
¼ tsp crushed red pepper
parsley (optional for garnish)

1) Wash all vegetables.
2) Using a steamer pot, heat 2 cups of water.
3) Using a paring knife, gently score an *x* on both ends of Roma tomatoes (you will just want to break the skin of the tomatoes and not cut into the flesh). Place scored tomatoes into steamer basket in pot and allow to steam for 2–3 minutes, just allowing the skin of tomatoes to peel.
4) Peel skin of tomatoes and set aside.
5) Using a knife, cut off ends of yellow squash, zucchini, and eggplants.
6) Using a mandolin or knife, cut yellow squash, zucchini, eggplant, and tomatoes into slices that are ⅛ inch thick. You should have about 30–40 slices of each vegetable. Save remaining ends and unused pieces of vegetables.
7) Place a large 12-inch oven-safe saucepan over medium heat then add 3 TBS of olive oil, onion, garlic, tomato paste, and diced tomatoes. Cook for about 3–4 minutes.
8) Add tomato skins and remaining yellow squash, zucchini, eggplant, and tomatoes to saucepan and cook for 4–5 minutes.
9) Add vegetable stock, basil, oregano, thyme, garlic powder, white pepper, and crushed red pepper to saucepan. Cook for 10 minutes.
10) Pour cooked vegetables into a blender and blend for 1–2 minutes or until a smooth sauce is formed.
11) Pour blended sauce back into saucepan and add salt and black pepper. Cook for 8–10 minutes.
12) Remove saucepan from heat and allow to slightly cool.
13) Using a spatula, form an even layer of sauce on the bottom of the saucepan.
14) Preheat oven to 375°F.
15) Using sliced vegetables, form a color pattern (red, yellow, green, purple) and layer slices in a circular-spiral pattern on top of sauce in saucepan. Repeat this pattern until all slices are used and multiple circles of vegetables have covered the pan. Start from the outside edge of saucepan and work your way in.
16) Once vegetables have covered sauce, sprinkle ¼ tsp of salt and ¼ tsp of black pepper and drizzle olive oil on top of vegetables.
17) Cut a circular piece of parchment paper to cover vegetable in saucepan.
18) Place saucepan in oven. Cook for 1 hour.
19) Remove saucepan from oven and remove parchment paper.
20) Drizzle a light amount of olive oil over vegetables.

Plating

Place ring mold in center of plate. Layer sliced vegetables inside in circular-spiral layers. Gently remove ring mold from dish. Using a small shallow bowl, place sliced vegetables inside in circular-spiral layers and turn onto plate.

Using a spoon, add desired amount of sauce to vegetables. Garnish with fresh basil sprig on the side and minced flat-leaf parsley.

Seared Lamb Chops with Mint Chimichurri and Smashed Potatoes

Lamb Chops
6 4 oz lamb chops
3 TBS olive oil
½ TBS garlic powder
½ TBS onion powder
1 tsp cayenne pepper
¼ tsp white pepper
¼ tsp black pepper
½ tsp salt
¼ tsp mustard powder
¼ tsp ground cumin
¼ tsp allspice

Smashed Potatoes
1½ LB multicolored gemstone potatoes
1½ TBS olive oil
1 TBS fresh rosemary (removed from
    stem and coarsely chopped)

1 TBS minced garlic
salt
black pepper

Mint Chimichurri
1 C mint leaves (finely chopped)
1 C flat-leaf parsley (finely chopped)
1 small jalapeño (seeded and chopped)
1 small Fresno chili (seeded and chopped)
1 small shallot (finely chopped)
1 TBS minced garlic
2 TBS red wine vinegar
½ C + 2 TBS olive oil
pinch of white sugar
salt
black pepper

Lamb Chops
1) Prepare lamb chops by cutting meat way from top portion of rib (about 4–5 inches) and leaving medallion at base of chops (4 oz portion).
2) Using 2 TBS of olive oil, rub down lamb chops. Prepare spice mixture in bowl by adding garlic powder, onion powder, cayenne pepper, white pepper, black pepper, salt, mustard powder, cumin, and allspice. Mix together to combine.
3) Season and rub in spice mixture on both sides of each lamb chop (about 1–1½ tsp per chop).
4) Heat cast-iron skillet over medium heat. Add 1 TBS of olive to skillet.
5) Once skillet is hot and lightly smoking, add 2 chops at a time to skillet. Cook for 2 minutes and then flip and cook for 3 minutes for medium-rare or 3½ minutes for medium. Remove lamb chops from skillet and repeat process for remaining lamb chops. Allow lamb chops to rest for 5 minutes before serving.

Smashed Potatoes
1) Boil 2 quarts of water in pot. Add about ½ TBS salt to water. Once water is boiling, add potatoes to pot and boil for 10 minutes.
2) Remove potatoes from pot and place in bowl and allow to cool for 5 minutes.
3) Add olive oil, rosemary, and garlic to bowl with potatoes. Add desired amount of salt and black pepper to bowl. Toss together until potatoes are coated.
4) Preheat oven to 350°F.
5) Place potatoes on a 12 × 17 baking sheet. Using a small flat-bottom glass, gently press down on potatoes to smash them into disk about ¼ inch thick.
6) Bake potatoes in oven for 20 minutes. Remove from oven and flip potatoes over and cook for another 10 minutes.
7) Remove from oven and allow to cool.

Mint Chimichurri
1) Add mint, parsley, jalapeño, Fresno chili, shallot, and garlic to a bowl and mix together.
2) Add red wine vinegar and olive oil to bowl and combine. Add salt and pepper to taste.
3) Allow to rest for 1 hour before serving. *(Do not place in refrigerator.)*

Plating

Spoon smashed potatoes onto plate and lay 2 lamb chops on side of potatoes. Finish with a lite drizzle of olive oil if desired. Serve mint chimichurri on the side in a small dipping cup to add desired amount to plate.

Seared Duck Breast with Glazed Rainbow Carrots

Duck Breast
2 7 oz duck breast
salt
black pepper
2 cloves garlic (smashed)
4–5 sprigs fresh thyme

Glazed Rainbow Carrots
16 oz baby rainbow carrots
salt
black pepper
1 TBS butter

1 sprig fresh rosemary
3–4 sprigs fresh thyme
2 TBS honey
2 TBS maple syrup
1 TBS water

Cranberry-Citrus Sauce
1 14 oz can whole cranberry sauce
¾ C orange juice
1 sprig fresh rosemary
4–5 sprigs fresh thyme
zest of 1 blood orange

Duck Breast
1) Heat a large cast-iron or oven-safe skillet over medium heat and preheat oven to 375˚F.
2) Using a fillet knife, score the skin of duck breast 3–4 times. Each score should be ¼ inch deep.
3) Season both sides of duck breast with desired amount of salt and black pepper (about ¼ each).
4) When skillet is hot, add duck breast skin side down. Add garlic and thyme to skillet as well. Allow to cook for 8–10 minutes to crisp skin.
5) Transfer skillet to oven and cook for 8–10 minutes for medium. Remove skillet from oven and keep warm.

Glazed Rainbow Carrots
1) Peel and wash carrots.
2) Place medium-sized pan on stove over medium heat.
3) Add butter, thyme, and rosemary to pan and cook for 1 minute. Add cleaned carrots to pan and toss with butter. Season with salt and black pepper. Cook for 3–4 minutes.
4) In a small bowl, combine honey, maple syrup, and water. Mix together. Drizzle mixture over carrots and toss tighter to coat carrots. Cook for 2–3 minutes. Remove from heat.

Cranberry-Citrus Sauce
1) Place a small saucepan over medium heat on stove. Add orange juice, cranberry sauce, and zest of blood orange to pan.
2) Using cooking twine, tie together rosemary and thyme sprigs. Add to pan to steep.
3) Bring mixture to a boil and then reduce heat to simmer. Cook down until mixture is about half, stirring occasionally (about 10–12 minutes). Remove from heat and allow to cool. Discard thyme and rosemary.

Plating

Slice duck breast into equal-size slices and place on plate. Arrange carrots in color pattern to display the different colors. Next, using a spoon, add cranberry-citrus sauce over sliced duck breast. Add a couple of sprigs of fresh thyme to plate for garnish.

Seared Stuffed Pork Chops with Apples and Pears

Brine
2 C cold water
1 C apple cider vinegar
3 TBS kosher salt
1 TBS whole black peppercorns
2 bay leaves
1 cinnamon stick
3 garlic cloves (smashed)

Ingredients
2 bone-in pork loin rib chops
    1" thick (8–10 oz each)

1 4 oz goat cheese (blueberry-flavored)
1 C apple cider vinegar
1 large Honeycrisp or Pink Lady apple
1 large Bosc pear
1 small yellow onion
4 garlic cloves
1 TBS canola oil
2 TBS honey
6 sprigs of thyme
salt
black pepper

Brine
1) Combine cold water, kosher salt, and 1 cup of apple cider vinegar. Mix together to dissolve salt in a gallon-sized ziplock bag. Once salt is dissolved, add whole black peppercorns, bay leaves, cinnamon stick, and garlic and mix together.
2) Add pork chops to brine and seal bag and allow to marinate for 1–2 hours in refrigerator.

Pork Chops
1) Remove pork from brine and gently pat pork chops dry. Next, using a fillet knife, split the pork chop in the middle, creating a pocket that reaches the bone. Once pocket is formed, add 2 oz of goat cheese to each pork chop and press down until pocket is closed. Season pork chops with salt and black pepper on each side.
2) Preheat oven to 350°F.
3) Place a large cast-iron skillet on stove top over medium-high heat.
4) Once skillet is hot, place pork chops in skillet and cook for 1 minute per side. Repeat this step so each side cooks twice.
5) Once pork chops have cooked twice per side, place in oven and cook for 10 minutes.
6) Using pot gloves, remove skillet from oven and check that internal temperature of pork chops has reached 140–145°F in the thickest part.
7) Remove pork chops from skillet.

Apple and Pears
1) Core apple and cut into ¼ inch slices, core pear and slice into ¼ inch slices, cut onion into ½ inch wedges, and peel and slice 4 garlic cloves.
2) Place skillet on stove with medium-high heat and add canola oil to skillet. Add onion and garlic to skillet and cook until onions begin to soften and brown (about 3–4 minutes). Add thyme sprigs, apples, pears, 1 cup apple cider vinegar, and 1 TBS honey. Toss together and cook for 2–3 minutes. Add a pinch of salt and black pepper.
3) Reduce heat to medium-low simmer and nestle pork chops into skillet with apple and pears. Allow to warm through for 2–3 minutes.
4) Remove skillet from heat. Using a brush, coat pork chops and apple-pears with 1 TBS of honey and finish with a pinch of salt and black pepper.
5) Add additional thyme sprigs for garnish (optional).

Rustic Spaghetti and Meatballs

Meatball
(yields 14–16 meatballs)

½ LB ground rib eye
½ LB ground veal or ground pork loin
2 large garlic cloves (minced)
½ shallot (minced)
1 large egg
½ C grated Romano cheese
1½ tsp chopped parsley
1 tsp chopped fresh oregano
1 tsp chopped fresh thyme
1 C Italian breadcrumbs
¾ C whole milk
½ C olive oil
salt
black pepper

Marinara Sauce
1 28 oz can crushed tomatoes
1 14 oz can diced tomatoes

1 6 oz can tomato paste
8 garlic cloves (sliced)
1 small yellow onion (diced)
1 tsp red pepper flake
1 tsp chopped fresh oregano
1 tsp chopped fresh thyme
1½ tsp chopped fresh basil
1 tsp salt
¼ tsp black pepper
¼ C olive oil
¼ C white wine

Additional Items
2–4 4–5 oz portions of fresh pasta (reserve
    ½ C of pasta water for each portion)
additional fresh basil
shredded or grated Parmesan cheese

Meatball
1) Combine ground rib eye and ground pork/veal into bowl and mix together.
2) Add garlic, shallot, Romano cheese, parsley, oregano, thyme, breadcrumbs, milk, olive oil, and egg and mix together.
3) Add desired amount of salt and pepper and mix together with mixture.
4) Cover and place bowl in refrigerator for 30 minutes.
5) Preheat oven to 400°F.
6) Remove bowl from refrigerator. Using spoon or hands, create golf ball–sized meatballs.
7) Place meatballs on greased bacing sheet.
8) Place in oven and bake for 20–25 minutes.
9) Remove from oven and set aside.

Marinara Sauce
1) Place stockpot on stove over medium-high heat.
2) Once pot is warm, add ⅛ C of olive oil to pot with garlic and onions. Sauté for 2–3 minutes or until onions are lightly translucent. Stir occasionally.
3) Add crushed tomatoes, diced tomatoes, and tomato paste to pot and mix together. Cook for 4–5 minutes. Stir occasionally.
4) Lower stove to medium-low heat. Add red pepper flakes, oregano, thyme, and basil. Mix together and cook for 3–4 minutes. Stir occasionally.
5) Transfer mixture to blender and blend until sauce is smooth.
6) Return sauce back to pan over low heat. Add ⅛ C olive oil, white wine, salt, and black pepper. Stir together and cook for 2–3 minutes.
7) Add prepared meatballs to sauce and cook for 4–5 minutes.
8) Remove from heat.

Serving Portion
1) In a pot, cook 1 portion of fresh pasta at a time.
2) Place a large saucepan over medium heat. Add ½–⅔ C of marinara sauce to saucepan with 4 meatballs.
3) Add cooked pasta to saucepan.
4) Add ½ C of pasta water to saucepan and stir together.
5) Heat for 1–2 minutes, stirring pasta and marinara together until pasta is coated in sauce.
6) Remove from heat.

Plating

Place a few spoonsful of sauce on the bottom of the plate. Using tongs, twist together pasta and place in center of plate over sauce. Place meatballs on sides of pasta and garnish as desired with fresh basil and/or Parmesan cheese.

Steak and Lobster with Crab Béarnaise

Steak
2 4 oz filet mignon
salt
black pepper
4 TBS butter
3 cloves garlic (smashed)
2 sprigs rosemary

Lobster
2 6 oz lobster tails
3 TBS butter (melted)
1 tsp salt
½ tsp black pepper
½ tsp garlic powder
½ tsp onion powder
¼ tsp paprika
1 tsp lemon juice

2 TBS white wine
2 TBS water

Crab Béarnaise
6 oz lump crabmeat (cooked)
¼ C white wine vinegar
½ small shallot (minced)
½ tsp black pepper
1 TBS tarragon (chopped)
2 egg yolks
8 TBS butter (melted)
1 TBS water
salt
lemon juice

Additional Items
cooked steamed asparagus

Steak
1) Preheat oven to 400°F.
2) Season all sides of steak with desired amount of salt and black pepper.
3) Place an oven-safe skillet on stove over medium-high heat with 1 TBS butter. Heat until pan starts to lightly smoke.
4) Place steak in pan and sear for 1 minute. Flip steak over and sear other side for 1 minute. Remove pan from stove and place in oven and cook for 8 minutes for medium cook.
5) Remove pan from oven and place on stove top over medium-high heat. Add 3 TBS of butter, garlic, and rosemary to pan. Allow butter to melt.
6) Tilt the pan halfway off burner. Using a pair of tongs, place garlic and rosemary on top of steak. Using spoon, baste the steaks in butter by continuously spooning butter on top of steak, garlic, and rosemary. Baste steak for 1 minute.
7) Remove steak from pan and place on a cutting board to rest. Using a meat thermometer, place probe in middle of steak to check temperature.

Cook	Internal Temperature	Time in Oven
Rare	125°F	3–4 minutes
Medium rare	135°F	4–5 minutes
Medium	145°F	7–8 minutes
Well-done	160°F	10–11 minutes

Lobster
1) Preheat oven to 450°F.
2) Using kitchen shears/scissors, cut down the middle of shell of lobster tails until ½ inch away from tail fin. Using a spoon, separate lobster meat from shell. Next, gently pull lobster meat up from tail and rest

lobster meat down on top of shell. Fold over top layer of lobster meat skin to expose inside of lobster. Place tails in an oven-safe pan.

3) In a small bowl, combine butter, salt, black pepper, garlic powder, onion powder, paprika,, and lemon juice. Mix together. Using a brush, brush each lobster tail with desired amount of butter seasoning.
4) Add white wine and water to pan with lobster tails.
5) Place pan in oven and bake for 12–15 minutes.
6) Remove pan from oven and allow lobster tails to rest for 2 minutes.

Crab Béarnaise
1) In a saucepan, add white wine vinegar, shallot, black pepper, and tarragon. Set pan over medium heat. Bring mixture to boil then lower heat and simmer for 5 minutes. Remove pan from heat and set aside to cool.
2) Fill another small saucepan with 1–1½ inches of water and set over medium-high heat. Once water begins to boil, lower heat to low to prevent water from boiling more.
3) Place cooled white wine vinegar mixture in a small metal bowl that will fit over top of saucepan with water. Add 1 TBS of water and egg yolks to bowl. Whisk together all ingredients in bowl.
4) Place bowl on top of pan with water. Be sure that the bottom of pan does not touch the water. Continue whisking egg yolks until mixture thickens (about 5–6 minutes). *Do not use an electric mixer.*
5) While still whisking mixture, slowly add butter. Add about 2 tablespoons at a time. Once all butter is added, remove bowl from pan. Continue whisking slowly until eggs and butter have emulsified. Once emulsion has formed, season with salt to taste and add a splash of lemon juice.
6) Add crabmeat to sauce and gently mix together to not break up the crabmeat.

Plating

Place cooked asparagus in a row on plate and place steak on top of asparagus. Place lobster tail on plate next to steak and asparagus. Next, spoon on crab béarnaise on top of steak (about 2–3 tablespoons). Serve.

Four-Cheese Basil-Spinach Stuffed Shells

Stuffed Shells
(yields 16 stuffed shells)

20 large pasta shells
4 oz baby spinach
¼ C fresh basil (chopped)
8 oz ricotta cheese
4 oz mascarpone
¼ C shredded mozzarella cheese
¼ C shredded Parmesan cheese
1 TBS minced garlic
½ medium shallot (minced)
1 TBS olive oil
⅛ tsp salt
⅛ tsp black pepper

Roasted Red Pepper Marinara Sauce
1 14 oz can crushed tomatoes

½ 14 oz can diced tomatoes
3 oz can tomato paste
½ C roasted red pepper (chopped)
4 garlic cloves (sliced)
½ small yellow onion (diced)
½ tsp red pepper flake
½ tsp chopped fresh oregano
½ tsp chopped fresh thyme
1 tsp chopped fresh basil
½ tsp salt
¼ tsp black pepper
2 TBS olive oil
2 TBS white wine

Additional Toppings
additional fresh basil
shredded Parmesan cheese

Stuffed Shells
1) Prepare pasta shells as directed by package.
2) Place a large saucepan with olive oil on stove over medium heat. Add garlic and shallot to pan and sauté for 2 minutes or until fragrant.
3) Add spinach and basil to pan and cook down until spinach is wilted (for about 2–3 minutes). Stir occasionally. Once wilted, remove from heat and transfer to cutting board. Roughly chop the spinach-basil mixture and allow to cool.
4) In a large bowl, add ricotta, mascarpone, mozzarella, and Parmesan cheese. Mix together until smooth. Once spinach-basil is cooled, add to bowl with cheeses and add salt and black pepper. Mix together until combined.
5) Transfer mixture to a piping bag.
6) Once pasta shells are cooled, gently pipe in 1–1½ TBS of mixture into each shell and place on baking sheet.

Marinara Sauce
1) Place stockpot on stove over medium-high heat.
2) Once pot is warm, add 1 TBS of olive oil to pot with garlic and onions. Sauté for 2–3 minutes or until onions are lightly translucent. Stir occasionally.
3) Add crushed tomatoes, diced tomatoes, tomato paste, and roasted red peppers to pot and mix together. Cook for 4–5 minutes. Stir occasionally.
4) Lower stove to medium-low heat. Add red pepper flakes, oregano, thyme, and basil. Mix together and cook for 3–4 minutes. Stir occasionally.
5) Transfer mixture to blender and blend until sauce is smooth.
6) Return sauce back to pan over low heat. Add 1 TBS olive oil, white wine, salt, and black pepper. Stir together and cook for 2–3 minutes.
7) Remove from heat.

Cooking Stuffed Shells
1) Preheat oven to 350°F.
2) Using a baking dish, add a few ladles of marinara sauce to bottom of dish and spread evenly. Next, place stuffed shells on top of sauce. Bake for 20 minutes.

Plating

Place a few tablespoonsful of sauce on the bottom of the plate. Using tongs, gently place 6 stuffed shells in center of plate over sauce. Garnish as desired with fresh basil and/or Parmesan cheese.

Spanish Paella

1½ C Spanish bomba rice or
   Italian Arborio rice
2 TBS olive oil
¼ red bell pepper (chopped)
¼ yellow bell pepper (chopped)
¼ green bell pepper (chopped)
½ yellow onion (chopped)
3 cloves garlic (minced)
4 oz ground chorizo sausage
2 mild Italian sausages with
   casing (sliced 1" thick)
½ LB boneless-skinless chicken
   breast (cut into ½" cubes)

½ LB peeled and deveined raw jumbo shrimp
½ LB mussels (cleaned)
½ LB little neck clams (cleaned)
½ C frozen peas
¼ tsp saffron threads
½ can fire-roasted tomatoes (14 oz can)
3 C chicken broth
½ tsp smoked paprika
1 bay leaf
2 TBS white wine
3 TBS flat-leaf parsley (chopped)
salt
black pepper

1) Place 12-inch paella pan or 12-inch cast-iron skillet over medium-high heat. Add olive oil to pan.
2) Add bell peppers, onion, and garlic to pan and sauté for 4–5 minutes or until onions are translucent. Lower heat to medium.
3) Lightly season cut chicken breast with salt and black pepper. Add chorizo, sausages, and chicken to pan and cook for 5–6 minutes or until chicken and sausage begin to brown. Stir pan often. Be sure to break up chorizo sausage as you stir.
4) Add rice and white wine to pan and stir together for 1 minute to coat rice. Next, add chicken broth, saffron, tomatoes, paprika, and bay leaf to pan. Stir together and bring pan to boil. Boil for 1 minute then turn down heat and simmer for 20 minutes. *Do not stir pan once it starts to simmer.* Give pan a couple of shakes to even out ingredients.
5) When rice has about 5 minutes left of cooking time, nestle clams, mussels, and shrimp into rice. Sprinkle frozen peas over dish too. Cover pan with lid or tinfoil. Cook for 5 minutes.
6) Once mussels and clams have opened up and shrimp is no longer translucent, remove pan from heat. Uncover pan and allow it to rest for 10 minutes.
7) Remove bay leaf from dish. Add salt and pepper to taste. Garnish with chopped parsley and serve. *Do not stir dish together.* Discard any mussels or clams that do not open up.

DESSERTS

Cookies 'n' Cream Mini Funnel Cakes

Funnel Cakes
(yields 8 mini funnel cakes)

1 C all-purpose flour
1 egg
¾ C + 2 TBS milk
¼ C melted butter
1½ TBS granulated sugar
2 tsp baking powder
⅛ tsp salt
¼ tsp vanilla extract
1½ TBS coco powder
1½ TBS crumbled chocolate sandwich
 cookies (10 cookies needed)

Chocolate Sauce
⅓ C milk chocolate chips
½ TBS coconut oil

White Chocolate Cookie Cream Sauce
sandwich cookie filling
¼ C white chocolate chips
½ TBS coconut oil

Optional Serving Ingredients
powdered sugar

Funnel Cakes
1) Place pot on stove over high heat and add 4–5 cups of vegetable oil. Heat to 300°F.
2) Using a knife, remove cream filling from chocolate cookie sandwiches. Save cream filling in a bowl. Place cookie halves into a bag. Crush cookies into fine crumble.
3) In a bowl, combine flour, baking powder, salt, sugar, and coco powder. Whisk together to combine. Once combined, add milk, egg, and vanilla extract. Whisk to incorporate with flour mixture. Next, whisk in melted butter. Lastly, add 1½ TBS of cookie crumble to batter and whisk to incorporate. Transfer batter to squeeze bottle with wide top or piping bag.
4) Once oil has reached temperature, place 2 3½ inch ring molds into oil with pair of tongs.
5) Inside each ring mold, squeeze batter, making a circular and zigzagging motion. About ¼ cup of batter will be used.
6) Once ring mold is filled, remove from oil with tongs and set aside. Allow funnel cakes to fry for 15 seconds then flip over using tongs and fry for another 15 seconds. Remove funnel cakes from oil with tongs and place on paper towel to dry. Repeat for remaining batter.

Chocolate Sauce
1) Add chocolate chips and coconut oil to a microwave-safe bowl. Place in microwave and cook for 30 seconds.
2) Remove bowl from microwave and stir together. Place back in microwave and cook for another 30 seconds. Remove and stir together.

White Chocolate Cookie Cream Sauce
1) Add reserved cookie filling, white chocolate chips, and coconut oil to a microwave-safe bowl. Place in microwave and cook for 30 seconds.
2) Remove bowl from microwave and stir together. Place back in microwave and cook for another 30 seconds. Remove and stir together.

Plating
Place funnel cakes on a tray in a few rows. Using a spoon, drizzle chocolate sauce over each funnel cake in a zigzagging motion. Drizzle desired amount. Repeat the same step for white chocolate cookie cream sauce. Transfer funnel cakes to plate and finish by sprinkling a few spoonfuls of remaining cookie crumble. Pour remaining sauces into small dipping cups if desired. (Optional: Using a small sift, sprinkle some powdered sugar onto plated funnel cakes.)

Note: This recipe makes for a fun waffle recipe.

Champagne-Infused Chocolate Strawberries

Strawberries
1 750 ml bottle of champagne
  or sparkling wine
10 medium or large strawberries
2 C milk chocolate chips
2 C white chocolate chips
2 C dark chocolate chips
3 TBS coconut oil

Optional Toppings
coconut flakes
chocolate sandwich cookies (crumbled)
Sugar in the Raw

Strawberries
1) Wash and clean strawberries. Place strawberries in a large container and pour champagne or sparkling wine in container with strawberries. Cover container and place in refrigerator for 6 hours.
2) Place each set of chocolate chips in separate glass bowls with 1 TBS coconut oil each. Place small saucepan with 1 C of water over high heat. Once water is boiling, place glass bowl over saucepan and stir chocolate chips to melt. Be sure to not let the bottom of glass bowl touch the water. Once chocolate is melted and smooth, remove from heat and set aside to cool. Repeat for each bowl of chocolate chips. Allow chocolate sauces to cool for 5–10 minutes, stirring occasionally.
3) Once chocolate sauces have cooled, pour 1½ C into small glasses. Reserve remaining chocolate sauces in bowls.
4) Remove all strawberries from container and gently pat dry and ensure they are completely dry.
5) When ready to dip strawberries, stick a skewer into the top of strawberries for easier dipping.

To Make Marble Swirl Strawberries
- Using reserved chocolate sauces and using a spoon, drizzle swirl and zigzag marks over chocolate sauces in glasses (for example, make swirl marks with reserved milk chocolate over glass of white chocolate).
- Next, while dipping strawberry into glass, turn strawberry in a clockwise motion until you are near top of strawberry. When bringing strawberry back up, reserve rotation in a counterclockwise motion. Place strawberries on parchment paper to set up.
- Repeat swirls over chocolate sauce before dipping next strawberry.

To Make Drizzled Strawberries
- Dip strawberry into chocolate sauce and place on parchment paper to set. Once strawberry has rested for 2–3 minutes, use a spoon and slowly drizzle strawberry with chocolate sauce starting from the bottom of strawberry, making a side-to-side motion.

For Topped Strawberries
- Once strawberry is dipped and placed on parchment paper, use a spoon to sprinkle the topping of choice over strawberry. Place strawberries in refrigerator and allow to set.

Glazed Donut Bread Pudding and Butter-Rum Caramel Sauce

Glaze Donut Bread Pudding
6 large glazed donuts
2 large eggs
2 egg yolks
2 C half-and-half
1 TBS sugar
1 TBS vanilla extract
¼ tsp salt
1 TBS cinnamon
¼ tsp ground nutmeg
⅛ tsp ground clove
butter

Butter-Rum Caramel Sauce
¼ C butter (½ stick)
½ C packed light brown sugar
¼ C half-and-half
1 TBS spiced rum

Additional Items
butter pecan ice cream or vanilla ice cream
2 large glazed donuts (torn into small pieces)

Bread Pudding
1) Preheat oven to 350°F.
2) Cut 6 glazed donuts into ⅛s. Place cut pieces onto parchment-lined baking sheet and place in the oven for 15 minutes. Remove from oven and allow to cool for 5 minutes.
3) To form custard base, use a blender to combine eggs, egg yolks, half-and-half, sugar, vanilla, salt, cinnamon, nutmeg, and clove. Blend together until fully combined and foamy (about 3–4 minutes); you may need to stop and scrape sides of blender once or twice.
4) Place cooled donut pieces in a large bowl and add custard base and toss together. Press down on donut pieces to submerge into custard base. Allow to sit for 5 minutes. After 5 minutes mix bowl again to combine donuts and custard. Press down again and allow to sit for 5 more minutes.
5) Use an 8 × 8 inch baking dish; use butter to grease baking dish.
6) Pour bread pudding mixture into greased baking dish and spread evenly.
7) Place 8 × 8 inch baking dish inside a larger baking dish. Fill larger baking dish with warm water halfway up the side of the 8 × 8 inch baking dish to create a water bath.
8) Place bread pudding in oven at 350°F for 1 hour.
9) Remove baking dishes from oven and remove 8 × 8 inch baking dish with bread pudding and set aside to cool for 10 minutes.

Butter-Rum Caramel Sauce
1) While bread pudding is cooling, place a small saucepan on stove over medium heat.
2) Cube butter and add to saucepan with brown sugar. Using a whisk, mix together butter and brown sugar until a smooth consistency is formed for about 5 minutes, stirring constantly.
3) Remove from heat. Next, add spiced rum and half-and-half to saucepan and whisk together to incorporate.
4) Allow sauce to cool for 10 minutes.

Plating
Using a 3½ inch diameter ring mold (or knife), cut out piece of bread pudding and place in mini cast-iron skillet or plate. Top with 1 scoop of ice cream and add a generous drizzle of caramel sauce to top of dessert. Finish by adding some torn pieces of glaze donut to dish.

Cinnamon Spice Cake with Berry-Peach Compote

Cake
1 16 oz white cake mix
¼ C white sugar
1 tsp ground cinnamon
½ tsp ground nutmeg
¼ tsp ground clove
1 tsp vanilla extract

Berry-Peach Compote
2 C frozen mix berries

1¼ C frozen peach slices
¼ C white sugar
1 TBS orange zest
1½ oz brandy
1 TBS cornstarch
3 TBS water

Additional Items
vanilla ice cream

Cake
1) Preheat oven to required temperature per cake package.
2) Prepare cake mix per package instructions. Add sugar, cinnamon, nutmeg, clove, and vanilla extract to cake batter and combine.
3) Pour cake batter into greased 9 × 9 inch metal baking pan. Bake for 25 minutes.
4) Remove cake from oven and allow to cool.

Berry-Peach Compote
1) Place a small saucepan on stove over medium heat.
2) Add frozen mixed berries, sugar, orange zest, and brandy to pan; stir together. Cook for 5–6 minutes, stirring occasionally.
3) After 5 minutes, lower heat to medium-low and add frozen peaches to pan. Stir to combine and cook for 2 minutes.
4) In a small bowl, combine cornstarch and water and whisk together.
5) Remove pan from heat and add cornstarch slurry to pan and stir together until fully incorporated.
6) All compote to cool for 10 minutes, stirring occasionally.

Plating
Using a square mold or knife, cut out a square 3 × 3 or 4 × 4 inch piece of cake and place in center of plate. Using a spoon, add 3–4 TBS of berry-peach compote on top of cake. Finish with a scoop of vanilla ice cream on top of berry-peach compote.

Poached Bosc Pears

4 Bosc Pears
1 750 ml bottle of Cabernet
   Sauvignon red wine
1 large cinnamon stick
1 TBS whole cloves
½ C fresh raspberries

¼ C white sugar
½ C orange juice
1 1 × 4 inch orange rind
vanilla ice cream
2 TBS chopped pecans

1) Peel pears and core bottom of pears. Be sure to leave stems on pears.
2) In a saucepan large enough to hold all 4 pears, add red wine, cinnamon stick, cloves, raspberries, sugar, orange juice, and orange rind. Place pan over medium-high heat and stir together.
3) Add pears to saucepan. Bring to a boil and boil for 5 minutes. Once boiling, reduce heat and simmer for 20 minutes. Stir pears around to ensure even poaching and color.
4) Remove saucepan from heat and cover saucepan and place in refrigerator to cool for 3 hours minimum.
5) Once pears have cooled, gently remove pears from liquid and set on plate. Strain liquid to remove cinnamon stick, cloves, raspberries, and orange rind. Return strained liquid to saucepan and place over high heat. Discard strained items. Bring liquid to a high boil and reduce liquid by half (about 20 minutes). Once reduced, remove pan from heat and allow to cool for 30 minutes.

Plating

Using a plate with shallow bottom, gently place pear on plate. Using a ladle, add about 4–5 TBS of cooled sauce over pear. Place one scoop of vanilla ice cream on plate next to pear. Finish with sprinkling ½ TBS of chopped pecans over pear and ice cream.

THE NEXT MORNING

Smoked Salmon Eggs Benedict

Eggs Benedict
2 English muffins
4 poached eggs
4 oz smoked salmon
1 small ripe avocado (peeled and sliced thinly)
1 oz sturgeon caviar (optional)
fresh dill weed sprigs

Hollandaise Sauce
4 egg yolks
8 TBS butter (melted)
1 TBS lemon juice
cayenne pepper
salt
black pepper

Hollandaise Sauce
1) In a stainless steel bowl, add egg yolks and lemon juice. Vigorously whisk together until mixture thickens and doubles in volume.
2) Place a saucepan over medium heat with 1 C water. Bring heater to a simmer. Place stainless steel bowl over saucepan and be sure water does not touch bottom of bowl.
3) While rapidly whisking egg mixture, slowly drizzle in melted butter to bowl until sauce thickens and doubles in volume (about 3–4 minutes). Remove bowl from heat.
4) Whisk in a pinch of cayenne pepper and add salt and black pepper to taste.
5) If mixture is too thick, whisk in a few drops of water at a time to desired consistency. Keep mixture in a warm place until ready to serve.

Plating

Slice English muffin in half and lightly toast. Place English muffin halves on plate and add ¼ of sliced avocado to 1 side of each English muffin half. Next, place 1 oz of smoked salmon on the other side of avocado. Using a spoon, gently place poached egg on top of salmon and avocado. Using a spoon, pour on 2–3 TBS of hollandaise sauce on top of each poached egg. Be sure not to smother the dish in sauce. Lastly, add 1 tsp of caviar to top of each half. Garnish dish with small dill weed springs.

Chicken and Waffles

Fried Chicken
(yields 8–10 wings)

2 LBS whole chicken wings
2¾ C all-purpose flour
1 TBS garlic powder
1 TBS onion powder
1 TBS cayenne pepper
1 tsp mustard powder
½ tsp paprika
1 tsp salt
½ tsp black pepper
¼ tsp ground thyme
3 C buttermilk

3 TBS Frank's RedHot sauce
¾ gallon vegetable oil

Waffles
(yields 6 waffles)

2 eggs
2 C all-purpose flour
1¾ C milk
½ C melted butter
1 TBS honey
4 tsp baking powder
¼ tsp salt
½ tsp vanilla extract

Fried Chicken
1) In a large bowl, combine buttermilk and hot sauce and mix together. Next, add chicken wings to buttermilk and cover and place in refrigerator for a minimum of 3 hours.
2) In a large bowl, combine flour, garlic powder, onion powder, cayenne pepper, mustard powder, paprika, salt, black pepper, and thyme and mix together to form dredge.
3) Remove chicken from refrigerator. One at a time, remove chicken from buttermilk (shaking off excess buttermilk) and dredge wing in flour mixture and coat all wing. Set aside. Repeat for all wings. Once all wings have been dredged, repeat process. Dip one wing into buttermilk and then dredge again and set aside. Repeat for all wings.
4) Add vegetable oil in a large pot over medium-high heat. Heat oil to 300–350°F (use a candy thermometer).
5) When oil has reached temperature, add 2–3 wings to oil slowly, ensuring wings are submerged in oil. Allow wings to fry for 9–10 minutes. Remove wings from oil and place on wire drying rack. Repeat until all wings are cooked. (Note: allow oil to come back up to temperature before adding next batch).

Waffle
1) In a large bowl, combine all-purpose flour, baking powder, and salt and mix together with whisk.
2) Next, add eggs, milk, melted butter, honey, and vanilla extract to bowl and whisk together.
3) Add ½ cup of waffle batter to waffle iron and cook to desired temperature/color.

Nashville Hot Chicken
Combine 1 C of cooled cooking vegetable oil, ½ C of Frank's RedHot sauce, 1 TBS cayenne pepper, and ½ tsp paprika to bowl and whisk together. Toss chicken wings in mixture and set aside.

Breakfast Quiche

Quiche
1 premade piecrust
4 eggs
½ C milk
½ C heavy cream
¾ C cooked bacon (crumbled)
½ C cherry tomatoes (cut in half)
4 oz baby spinach

1 scallion (sliced thinly)
¼ tsp mustard powder
1 TBS olive oil
salt
black pepper
1 C shredded cheddar cheese
2 TBS all-purpose flour

1) Preheat oven to 400°F.
2) Prepare piecrust per package directions.
3) Place a large pan on stove over medium heat. Add olive oil to pan and heat for 30 seconds. Add spinach to pan and cook down, stirring constantly. Cook for 2–3 minutes or until spinach has wilted. Remove from heat and allow to cool.
4) In a large bowl, add eggs milk, heavy cream, and mustard powder. Whisk all ingredients together until smooth. Season with salt and black pepper.
5) In a separate bowl, add cheese and flour. Toss together until cheese is coated with flour.
6) Using a 9-inch pie dish, roll out piecrust and pinch edges.
7) Layer cheese mixture on into piecrust. Next, add spinach and tomatoes to dish and spread evenly. Next, add bacon and scallions to dish and add evenly.
8) Slowly pour egg mixture into dish to cover all ingredients. *Do not fill higher than pie crust.*
9) Using tin foil, cover edges of piecrust. This prevents the crust from burning.
10) Place quiche into oven and bake for 1 hour. With 10 minutes remaining, remove tin foil from piecrust edges.
11) Remove quiche from oven and allow to cool for 10 minutes before cutting for serving.

Vegetarian Alternative

If you desire to make this a veggie quiche, you can substitute bacon with ¾ C chopped white mushrooms and ¼ C broccoli. Cook mushrooms and broccoli with ½ TBS olive oil for 5 minutes over medium heat or until mushrooms just begin to soften.

French Toast

1½ tsp ground cinnamon
½ tsp ground nutmeg
¼ tsp ground clove
3 TBS white granulated sugar
3 TBS melted butter
4 eggs
¼ C milk
½ tsp vanilla extract
8 1-inch slices of French bread
½ C warmed maple syrup

Whipped Cream
1 C heavy whipping cream
1 tsp vanilla extract
2 TBS granulated white sugar

Optional Toppings
1 TBS powdered sugar
blueberries
strawberries
chopped pecans

French Toast
1) Mix cinnamon, nutmeg, clove, sugar, and butter together in a bowl.
2) Crack 4 eggs in bowl with milk and vanilla and whisk until incorporated.
3) Add butter-spice mixture to eggs and whisk together.
4) Transfer batter to shallow pie dish. Heat griddle top or pan over medium heat.
5) Dip sliced bread into batter and coat both sides of bread.
6) Add coated bread to warmed griddle top and cook for 1–2 minutes per side or until golden brown.
7) Remove French toast from griddle top to plate to allow to cool.

Whipped Cream
1) Place medium-sized metal bowl in freezer for 10–15 minutes.
2) Remove chilled bowl from freezer and add heavy whipping cream, sugar, and vanilla extract.
3) Using a hand mixer on medium speed, mix together ingredients until cream forms stiff peaks.

Blueberry-Lemon and Cranberry-Orange Scones

Scone Base
(yields 4 scones)

1 C all-purpose flour, plus extra
¼ C granulated sugar
½ TBS baking powder
2 TBS cold butter
2 TBS cream cheese
1 small egg
¼ C sour cream
½ tsp vanilla extract
pinch of salt
turbinado or raw sugar

Blueberry-Lemon
½ C frozen blueberries
2 TBS lemon zest
1 C confectioners' sugar
1 TBS lemon juice
3 TBS milk

Cranberry-Orange
½ C frozen cranberries
2 TBS orange zest
1 C confectioners' sugar
1 TBS orange juice
3 TBS milk

Scone Base
1) Preheat oven to 400°F. Line a baking sheet with parchment paper or Silpat.
2) In a large bowl, combine flour, sugar, baking powder, and salt and whisk together.
3) Cut cold butter into small cubes. Add butter and cream cheese to bowl, and using a pastry cutter or two forks, cut butter and cream into flour mixture.
4) In a small bowl, combine egg, sour cream, and vanilla. Whisk together until combined.
5) Pour wet mixture into flour bowl and combine using a soft-tipped spatula. *Do not overmix* or the scones could be tough. Dough should take on a wet and tacky consistency.
6) Add in berries and 1 TBS of zest of choice. Fold into mixture with spatula.
7) Sprinkle flour onto clean smooth surface. Also coat hands with flour to help prevent sticking.
8) Turn mixture onto floured surface and knead dough into a 6-inch round circle that is about ½-inch thick.
9) Using a large knife, cut dough into 4 equal pieces. Separate the pieces, and using hands, gently form pieces into even triangles.
10) Using a flat spatula or pie turner, transfer scones to lined baking sheet. Space scones 2 inches apart on baking sheet.
11) Sprinkle each scone with about 1 tsp of turbinado or raw sugar.
12) Place scones in oven and bake for 20–25 minutes or until scones are lightly golden brown.
13) Remove from oven and allow to cool on pan for 5 minutes. Next, transfer scones to cooling rack to cool for about 8–10 minutes.

Scone Glaze
1) While scones are baking, in a medium-sized bowl, add confectioners' sugar, 1 TBS of zest of choice, juice of choice, and milk. Whisk together until smooth glaze is formed.
2) Once scones are cooled, dip the tops of scones into glaze until tops are coated. Place back on rack to allow glaze to set for 2–3 minutes.

EXTRAS

Fresh Pasta

2 C all-purpose flour, plus extra
1 TBS olive oil
2 large eggs

6 large egg yolks
pinch of salt

1) In a bowl, combine eggs, egg yolks, olive oil, and salt. Gently whisk together. *Do not overbeat.*
2) On a clean surface, add 2 cups of flour and create a well in center of flour.
3) Gently pour egg mixture into well of flour.
4) Using a fork, work in flour from well into egg mixture. Once flour is incorporated into eggs, flour hands and knead dough together for 8–10 minutes, ensuring all flour and egg is incorporated.
5) After kneading dough, you should have a slightly springy dough ball. Wrap dough in cling wrap and set aside to rest for 30 minutes at room temperature.

Forming Pasta Sheets
1) Flour work surface and remove dough from cling wrap and place on floured surface.
2) Using a bench knife, cut dough into 4 equal portions. Take each portion of dough and form uniform circle with dough.
3) Using a pasta sheeter or rolling pin, flour dough and roll out into sheets that are 6 inches wide and 2 feet long. Sheets should be $\frac{1}{16}$ inch thick.
   - If using pasta sheeter, start on number 1 setting and work your way down to number 7 or 8 setting to achieve $\frac{1}{16}$ inch thickness.
4) Lightly flour both sides of pasta sheets and set aside.

Forming Spaghetti Noodles
   - Electric cutter: Place desired pasta cutter attachment onto pasta cutter. Run formed pasta sheets through cutter at slow speed. Once pasta is cut, lightly flour pasta noodles and set aside until ready to cook.
   - Cutting by hand: Cut prepared pasta sheet in half to form 2 sheets. Gently fold sheet ends to meet in the middle to form 2 halves. Using a sharp knife, cut sheets to desired width of pasta noodles. Be sure to cut both halves at the same time. Then gently toss cut noodles with a little flour and set aside until ready to cook.

How to Poach an Egg

1) Place a saucepan with 3–4 C water over medium heat. Bring water to a low simmer. Add 1 TBS white vinegar to water and mix together.
2) Once water is simmering, crack egg into a small dish. Using a large spoon, create a vortex in the water and stir water in clockwise direction. Once vortex is formed, slowly place small dish into vortex and pour egg into water. Egg white will form a pouch around egg yolk. Allow egg to poach for 3–3½ minutes.
3) Using a slotted spoon, remove poached egg from water and place on soft towel to dry and cool for 1 minute. *Do not use paper towel.*
4) Repeat for remaining eggs.

CPSIA information can be obtained
at www.ICGtesting.com
Printed in the USA
BVHW020349150321
602456BV00003B/20